THE INNOCENT AND THE MERCILESS

Auna Raunea

Order this book online at www.trafford.com
or email orders@trafford.com

Most Trafford titles are also available at major online book retailers.

Author Credits:
i do good deeds as much as i can. i do the can drives. car washes
for the schools, chilie suppers for the schools.

Printed in the United States of America.

ISBN: 978-1-4269-6275-2 (sc)
ISBN: 978-1-4269-6276-9 (hc)
ISBN: 978-1-4269-6277-6 (e)

Library of Congress Control Number: 2011904682

Trafford rev. 04/28/2011

 www.trafford.com

North America & international
toll-free: 1 888 232 4444 (USA & Canada)
phone: 250 383 6864 ♦ fax: 812 355 4082

I never felt like I was human, or important to me or anyone. All I had was my special Education friends of us five girls, and our most loved teacher in the world. I would try so hard to get attention, I thought if I got noticed that they could see what my father was doing to me. My Father would get disappointed when I wasn't in bed with them in the morning. He would make threats to me if I would say I don't want to, My Father said that he makes me hot, and I feel good when it's over. If I made too much of a problem, He would tell me that I couldn't see my grandpa or grandma. But then he would tell me don't you tell grandpa or grandma our secret. I felt like it was my duty or what I was supposed to do. I ask all the time to go and play with different girls, but this man who brought beer to the bar said I wasn't good enough. He said I was a whore from a bar. I went to a school next door across the street to play with a girl, her mother said get away from my daughter you nasty little tramp. (I was 9yrs. Old) my father would always want me to go home with him, he would say he forgot something, my mother would say don't be too long looking for it, then she would have a smug look on her face. I would cry the whole time. My father got so mad he would take me back to our pizza and bar restaurant and say get the hell out of the car. I would be sore, and red, and hurting. I wanted to die all the time. We went to the drive inn I layed down in the back of the station wagon, and my father layed back on his elbow, and had his fingers inside my panties rubbing my personal place. Then he went to the bathroom. every morning I would be in his bed him rubbing, touching, and getting white stuff all over me. I was always told I was ugly, stupid, worthless, and nothing. I was told that I was a mistake, a brown spot on the mattress. My mother said that she had to bring into the world a retard. I was told by my father that he never loved me at all. I was a tax rite-off. That I would never amount to anything at all. My father couldn't get enough of touching me he said that it felt so good. It would hurt so much that I had a hard time sitting in school. I always had a change of clothes at the school or the school would call my mother to bring them to the school. I had bladder and kidney problems all the time. I didn't, and the doctor didn't know why my bladder and kidney's would make me go pee all the time. Sometimes without warning, my mother would yell and get so mad when she had to bring me clothes to the school. She would that she should make me wear them all day long to teach me a lesson. The kids at school heard this and from then on I got to be their target miss pee pants. It was hard enough being in special ed, and going threw what I had to live with. My teacher told my parents if you work with her she could be put in regular class room, later on, even a professor at the university said this too. My mother had to take me to the doctor, before we got there she said let me do the talking. The doctor said why is she so red in her private place (I can't remember the big word he used) she takes baths, the doctor said don't let her sit in the water the next time. So the next time my mother took me she told the doctor that I fell on my bike, after that my mother told the doctor she fell on a rail. My mother stop taking me to the doctor. Another doctor was ask to take my files, he saw that I hadn't been for 8 to 9 yrs. The doctor called and ask to speak to my mother, she argued with the doctor, then she said fine I will send her. My mother said you had better not say anything, my father said keep your goddamn mouth shut or you won't have a goddamn house to come back home too. I went there, and got a thing called look me all over. So I waited he came in the room and said why aren't you in a gown? I said you told me you just wanted to look at me. No I will be back, I said its okay I can just change here now, the doctor looked at me and said he will be out the door. The doctor checked me out and said to me are you washing the soap off good, I said yes I do when I take a bath. You have redness, and look very irritated. I got scared and lied, and told him that I took a bath. The doctor said okay that's why you have such irritated skin and that is why you are so red. He told me no more baths. When I got home my parents said what did you say. My father said don't you tell me a goddamn lie. I came home from the doctor and told my parents that I told the Doctor that I took baths, and he told me no more baths. My mother said you know this is your fault, you shouldn't look pretty, or wear pretty clothes if you would not resist you wouldn't get red. Your Father just wants to show you love. You seduced your father since you were two yrs. Old. We never had a family, no trust, no affection, never showed emotion, just going threw are own world each one of us. Everytime Our Father had to get us shoes he would say these goddamn kids aren't worth all this goddamn money. All I wanted was a chance at life growing up and being somebody. I was sitting on the toilet my father said that nice soft white bottom was his. My father got big in his underwear. He winked and said here hold it tight. I know if I said no he would get so mad. I was trying to make a bowel movement. When he left I finished, and saw worms in my poop, I said mother come look there is worms, she said I am not sending you to the doctor for that, they will go away by them selves. I got a bladder and kidney infections and before I pleaded with my mother that I couldn't pee my father said if she can't pee then she just might die. My father said no more of his goddamn money would be used on a goddamn retard. My father said to me go get in the goddamn car. I got a growth growing from my left eye into my right eye. I had to have an operation, my father said more goddamn money spent out of his goddamn money used on this worthless retard. Let this goddamn kid go goddamn blind. I had the operation, the doctor wanted 6 hundred dollars up front. My dad said when he was leaving he would get the goddamn 6 hundred dollars. I was at school once and fainted running the track, I fainted in the girls locker room and hit my head, the office called and told my parents to take me to the hospital to be checked. My parents put on a act until they got me in the car, and said we are not spending anymore goddamn money on you. You can fall asleep and die in your goddamn sleep. My parents tried to give me away to a neighbor so they wouldn't have to deal with me or spend anymore money. My father wanted to be alone with me all the time for sex, and his own sexual needs. My father said that your mother isn't as fresh as I was anymore. My father said he liked that tight, softed, fine hair bottom. When I got older he said I had the nicest breast he had ever saw. My father would play with my pink nipples while he had his hard thing between my legs. My father told me that it wouldn't be long and he could be inside me playing with my soft white breast, and my pink nipples. I was almost 14 yrs. Old. He didn't want to get me pregnant because he was afraid of going to jail. My father said we have to keep this quite our little secret. My mother and father told me everyone would blame me, since everyone knew my parents. No one would ever believe me anyway because your in retard room. My father said that he could kill me and they would never find my body. When I was in bed with my father my mother said lye still and it won't hurt anymore it will feel good and warm, you will like it. This friend that my father knew said to me he would and could kill me. He took me to a park and grabbed my neck real tight and unzipped his pants force his thing in my mouth and got white stuff in it and on my shirt, he told me to spit it out on the ground. He told me that I was his play toy. My father told this friend to have fun with me. Just don't get her pregnant. This friend would take me to his house as much as he could. He told me that my father told him she is soft and fresh. When I would go play in the neighborhood I didn't want to come back, but where would I sleep, eat, so I would go home. My mother would find any reason to get rid of me. My father when he would get threw he also would tell me to get lost. Until he needed more. My sister's son threw the bathroom door open and said to me that I have a hairy ass. When my sister's son was born my brother-in-law told my sister to not let me the retard around his son, because my retarded could rub off on his son. My sister told me the noise the water makes going down the drain is the drain monster, and will pull me down the drain and eat me all up. My sister said the red on pizza's is blood. I was always told that I was adopted, and they never wanted me, because I was fat, ugly, and retarded, and stupid. I was told by my father that he never wanted any of us at all, but especially my brother and I because we were in retarded school. I was always told that I was abandon, and left on the door stop like a bitch left me for them to care for. You told me that you only loved yourself in the family not me because I would never amount to anything. That they felt sorry for me and I wasn't thiers at all. I'm not important to you or anyone's life. I never felt love at all. Just their property they use when they want to, at their own discretion.

The innocence's and the merciless

I was two years old when my life began and ended. I pushed and kept any and all thoughts and memories down as deep as I could I wouldn't show emotions always on the defiance side of things.I never trusted anyone at all. I would never want to be involved. On the outside looking in. a little black boy would chase me, and my father said that he would kill that little monkey and me too, he told me he would put us in a potatoe sack and drown us. My life in a violent and hate atmosphere was a way of life, as I knew it. I would sit and wonder why god hated me so much. I wished that I was never born. My father would beat us when he wanted to, because we had to learn. My Father would back-hand us if we did or said the wrong thing, or not to his liking. He would give us a choice either the belt, houseshoe, or a fist, or his hand. Sometimes it would be for no reason. My Father would come home drunk. My Father told me that I wasn't worth the price of steak. When my Father would pick a fight with my brother My Father would beat my brother and I would have to get in-between them, and take a few punches. One time my Father punched me in the shoulder so hard I was hit so hard that I couldn't use my arm for 3 or 4 days. I never wanted to be involved because I got tired of being my Father's punching bag but I loved my brother, and it was okay by me to take some punches. My Father hit so hard it knocked me back 10 feet. One time my Father beat my brother because he had refused to do the dishes at the restaurant that my Father and Mother owned. My brother begged our Father to stop slapping him. My other brother left he couldn't watch it anymore. I would say to my Mother help she would say how could she nothing was wrong. My Mother would always get a certain look in her eyes, then she would say my little retard. I could never get love from my Mother because there wasn't any. All my Mother could see is herself and how everything affected her. Everything was a mirrow to my Mother. She was very dark inside and sick minded. My Mother wanted to paint the house inside walls to ceiling, and floors black. My Father would belittled me and made me feel as low as he could on a day-to-day schedule. All I was is a tax right off. He would always tell me that the best part of me ended up as a stain on the bed sheets, and the rest rolled down my Mother's ass-crack. My Father told me that my Mother didn't give birth to me she shit me out of her ass. This is what my Father would say to me that he should put me in a potatoe sack tie it and throw it in the river he would say this all the time. He would always threaten to kill my dog Murphy so he could see me cry, because I spend more time with Murphy then my Father and Mother to have love. My dog Murphy was my friend, companion, and my best friend, he always understood, me and my pain, I loved him so much. Growing up I never had a chance I never had anyone to talk to to love me, or listen to my cries for help but Murphy. The first time my Father did bad things to me was putting his hands, fingers, and his penis on and against my bottom, and on my personal place. I will never find love or be happy, I will always be in the shadow to try to be unnoticed. I am a empty shell always dead. My sister and brother in law hogged tied me and left me in a dark room for two and half hours with wet and soiled clothes. I yelled until one of the renters found me and untied me. He went down staires and told what he found, my Father and Mother put on a convincing act so he would be conned into believing they both were concerned. My Father touching me and putting his fingers inside went on none stop. My Father and his best friend enjoyed me day in and day out, non stop with touching, fingering me putting me down on my knees to have me open my mouth to both of them, and having me bend over the couch to sodmize me when they wanted, cussing me when it was my time of the month. My Father's best friend told me that he could kill me and get away with it because he was not scared I was always told this. I grew up with loose sheets and maybe one or two covers, or sleep on a bare mattress. I had a bladder problems and I wet the bed all the time. I was made to sleep on the floor and cover up with the clean clothes on the floor. I would ask for a half of a sandwich because I got use to eating less. I never could eat a whole sandwich, that was too much. My Father said to me you are going to eat a whole sandwich or I will shove it down your throat. My Father did just that I could not breathe and I was choking, I vomited up everything I just ate. My Father said that he should beat the dog shit out of me. My Mother made me watch a puppy choke to death on a chicken bone, that still haunts me to this day. I wanted to leave but my Mother would tell me of all the bad people in the world, and I was safe living there, nothing was wrong being with your Father and I. Sometimes I would have tears but not as much anymore. I got good to never listening to what I was told, because I learn to close my ears, this became a normal life to me. I wanted out so much, but I didn't know how. Then I would bring home animals to give them bread, milk, and eggs to eat on their long trip to find love. I wanted a new family, so I thought that I would go to a lawyer with fifty dollars and hire him, to find me a new family, I thought that fifty doallrs was like having a million dollars in my hand back then. I thought that it was the same as writing to santa, would find me a new family. I was told that I was stupid, and I would never be anything, but a loser. To my Father and Mother I will never forget what you said. I will never forget what you did. But I will always remember how you made me feel.

I was chasing something that was never there in the first place. My Father on a Friday in the summer months of the 70's told me my uncle was bringing horses to our house for me to ride. My Father told me to stay home all day Saturday and Sunday. I stayed home both days waiting for the horses to come. Sunday at 5:00pm I said where are the horses? My Father said to me that I was a stupid bitch to think my uncle is going to drive all the way down here for 4 hrs. Just to bring horses to you to ride. My Father looked at my Mother and said she is such a retard. He would always cry and say that he is sorry, and that it will never do it again. I thought that this was going to be my life forever. I was in the 3rd grade when a boy in my class started touching me when I was 8yrs. Old, it didn't stop until I was 9yrs. Old. One of my brother's caught us, he wasn't mad at me, he knew the reason why, because he knew what our Father and Mother had been doing with me before this happened. And my brother told us it was wrong we were too young to be doing that, my brother hugged me and said it's okay, just don't do it again, I told my brother that I touched him too. I took my anger out on a cat putting a string around his tail, and sliding the cat in a circle as fast as I could. I saw that I hurt the cat. I cried and said to god I will never hurt another animal again. In my house I was given a bath not a shower like I was suppose to get and this care giver put their fingers inside me. I started to say something, and this care giver told my Father that I wouldn't let her give me a bath. So I got a beating for it. When I came in the room this care giver said quietly said please don't tell. My Father would go out with his red neck friends and go nigger hunting in the 1960's said that their would a whole lot of niggers floating down the goddamn Mississippi river. My Father had me and another sister collect the rent at our family business, and we knocked on the door of an apartment and the man was standing there without clothes on, I was 9yrs. Old, and I ran down the stairs. I went to tell my Father and said that we were useless retards. My Father said he would get someone else to do the job because we couldn't do it right anyway. I went to my play day at school and got 3rd place. My Mother looked at me and in front of all the other Mothers she said couldn't you do better than that. I would have a retard, loser, disgrace, and a idiot for a daughter. Sometimes when my Mother was opening up the restaurant, she would look at me a say why can't you fix your own breakfast, and take care of your needs by yourself. She would also say this to me I guess I have to take you to school now, she would say I don't know why you are such a disappointment to be in the dumb class, just like all the rest of the degenerates in that class. When I thought that things were getting better I got knocked down again.I think that I also deserved love too. I would pray to god to come and get me but he never did I always wondered why. I was two years old when my Grandma got me a new dress, socks, shoes, panties, and t-shirts with fancy strapes. I was dancing outside in a circle. I was so proud and happy. I felt brand new. I remember it like it was yesterday. One of a few happy times. My Father told me to come into the house he wanted to show me something he said, so I hurried inside. I thought that he had something pretty for me, because he knows I like the light color of pink. Plus he was My father. So I went inside the house so excited. My Father told me to get on top of the table, and dance in a circle. I said Mother would get real mad. He said let me deal with that. So I got on the table like he told me, and started dancing in circle like he wanted. My Father started rubbing his hands on my legs, and started rubbing up farther and farther. He put his hands in my underwear and started putting his fingers inside me, he ripped my new clothes that I got from my grandma. My Father ripped my dress, underwear, and put his thing between my legs against my personal place. He got his white stuff all over me, and my new clothes. He told me to tell everyone that I fell off the porch. He told me to tell my Grandma the same story. And I had not say anything different, because he could kill me anytime, and get rid of me, and nothing would be done or said. He told me he has power, and lots of friends that would help him.Every morning he would put me in bed with him and my Mother. She would say to my Father you really shouldn't do those things to or with her, told my Father what would the neighbors think if she started getting a big stomach. Then she said well I am tired, and roll over the other way and go to sleep, I guess I will have to train her better, my Mother said. My Father would sit me on his lap and I could feel something hard then he would bounce me up and down on his lap. Then my Father would put me down and go in the bathroom at the restaurant, and bar that my Father and Mother owned. My Father would be in the bathroom along time. My Father would squeeze my bottom, and my thighs while I was in his lap when he was hard, and bouncing me. My Father would have me hold his thing real tight, and he would move me up and down, and back and forth until his white stuff would come out. My sister and brother-in-law hog tied me, and left me in a dark room with wet and soiled clothes for 2 and half hours, knowing how afraid I was of the dark. My brother-in-law called me to his apartment at the university and forced me to have sex with him. My Father would touch, and rub me everyday, he would say this is how much he loves me. I didn't know where to go are who to tell, even I thought that it must be okay. There was nothing and I was scared all the time. I thought that was what Fathers did with their daughters.

So I believed that it was okay. I just wanted to be loved and accepted. When my Grandpa died this was the worst day of my life. No more feeling safe, or having a safe zone, or my grandma's oatmeal and raisen, and pecan cookies, or listening to them pray the rosary, or saying the lords prayer, or saying hail mary's prayer. My grandpa and grandma's we would watch 60 minutes together and watch sports or our favorite TV shows in the 60's. My Father and his best friend had been touching me then they both raped and sodomized me for 2 and half hours this happened two weeks before my 16th birthday in the summer time in the 70's. I wanted this bad boy I dated to help me and come and get me so that I could hide, then everything would be okay. Even though my Father was all over me I still had my virginity my self of being pure for marriage, I would have to tell who I marry that I had been touch, and that I have seen a man naked. My Father and his best friend wouldn't have gotten the chance to rape and sodmize me. If that bad boy would have hid me. After that my father wore a condom he was not wanting me pregnant I was menstruating, or as my Grandma would say I have a vistor staying for a few days. He told me he had enough goddamn children. I could have got threw the touching, rubbing, and all the hitting, cussing coming out of church. After My Father and his best friend got threw and done with me the damage had been burned into my brain. When my Father and his best friend took away my virginity, I should have died. The thing is no one in our town would have believed me, because my Father and his best friend were leaders in the town. I didn't want to be stripped of more of my dignity. I wish that I would have been strong enough to take my own life. My world as I knew it is gone and was gone. To myself and me I couldn't admit it to myself that I wasn't a virgin anymore. I thought that if I went to a doctor he could make me a virgin again. I tried to save money to get away but my Father and Mother would steal it from me. When I was being made to touch and hold my Father's thing I didn't want to, it was gross. When my Father would make me look at his thing I didn't want to he would get so mad he would either hit, punch, or slap me. I was always thinking why. I had multiple thoughts of people on the inside of me, I hoped they would love me. I was in another world while all of this was going on. My Father would put his thing in my mouth so hard that he hurt my throat. My Father would make me put his thing in my mouth until he was done, then he would rape me, then sodomize me this was everyday if not every other day. I went in my room and dropped on to the bed and cried so hard I vomited. I hurt in ways I can't even begin to explain to all of you that read my story. People from good families can begin to comprehend. My Father brutalized our intire family and my Mother wasn't any better. People just don't get it or understand the shame, fear, pain, or hurt felt everyday. My Father and Mother thought that I was in special ed, and I wouldn't remember. I have a memory like an encyclopedia. What happened is all the disgusting things that happen were burnt in my brain, that helped when I got older and my brain got smarter and started remembering, and bring it all back so I started remembering back to when I was 2 years old. I asked my Aunt who lives, and lived in the south if I got a job could I come and live there. I was so powerless at this time. I was never wanted or important at all. The abuse from so many people was tremendous. Alone most of my life even though there was so many of us in the house was the hardest thing that we had to endure. My Mother was tired of dealing with me , and the rest of my family living there, and tired of raising children, I don't know when she ever did anything of that raising us she never wanted us at all. After the years of rape, sodomy, and the abuse, and the neglect this changed me for life. My Father and Mother would tell me and the others why don't you just walk in the middle of the interstate, maybe you would get hit. I had nothing and I will always feel that way down in my heart in that deep dark place of my soul I have lived there with absolutely no understanding of any kind of what my life was all about, or suppose to be about.Or what is the reason for my existence or my being here, what purpose was I to anyone. All I remember during what was supposed to be about the birth of chirst, when celebrating Christmas was cussing, yelling, hiting, and screaming. All I wanted at that time we all were going threw was during my whole lifetime, and the other children's lifetime was wanting to just die as fast as we could, or to just get away, and go away. I could have gotten help, and got threw step by step, but not after raping me and sodmizing me. I wish that they would have put a bullet to the back of my head. My husband told me he is not worth my time, but it still hurts a lot.This has caused me great pain, hurt, and sorrow in my life. I had 4 marriage proposals before I met my husband. Sometimes I would wet on myself until I was in my late 20's. I am a empty shell always dead. All I wanted was to be like the normal kids. I love my anger. I would love to have that sword with me, slice off some privates. Immensly would enjoy loving to watch him run in the prison yard with the bull-queers drooling behind him. I'm a very angry person. Love is just a made up word and nothing else. My anger controls me I get mad because my Father died, and I can't kill him anymore. Some one that was supposed to protect me used me. Being used and left to die a slow death is worse. I can't do anything to the one that is still alive. Trust no one! I tried writing a letter to both of my attackers it didn't work for me. I have road rage all the time. I am ready at the drop of a hat. When I feel anger boiling I walk or listen to hard rock and roll. My Father would always say children should be seen, but not heard. My Mother would ignore me, she would say to me she is having her moment to go away snot nosed bratt. There is no trust when it comes to me, never. Doubt in my life was normal to me. I try to hard to win people over, I guess I am stupid. I have tried to have a normal sex life. I feel like I don't exist. I have such anger toward my sister-in-law that one time she made me so pissed that I grabbed her and I almost slapped her for calling me incompetent. I don't know how I stopped myself before I hurt her real bad. I am afraid to lose control. I could kill the one attacker that is still alive. I keep my anger down deep as I can, with a liquid nail lid on it. I have been told I am a ticking time bomb. I like sometimes to be isolated. I will never get close or let someone get close to me. This is my real thoughts and feelings inside my mind. When I started talking about this to everyone I was shocked to see tears, crying, I didn't know that their would be concern for me. I don't enjoy sex or anything about it, because my husband is too big. I can still smell in my nose my Father's body odor, and cologne. I close my eyes and wake up screaming stop, no. I have even looked for a new wife for my husband instead of me, then she can step in where I left off. I am a cold-hearted bitch, and mad, rude, and I don't give a damn attitude. I have never felt good about me. I don't like hugs or kisses or people getting to close to me. No one wants to hear about this anymore, because no body cares. I don't drink it makes me a different person. I tried to shoot myself they put me in a Hospital. I don't want to love anymore people that's too much for me. I don't do good with too many people. Just my husband, son, daughter, son-in-law, and my grandson, okay that's enough people.

I never show weakness, I will put on a really good front so people won't see the real me. I run and hide. I put my feelings into check so no one sees the real me. Show none of yourself, and go unnoticed. Crying in front of people no way my walls just might come down on me too hard for me to handle. I can't do it, and I will not let it happen. I am living in a dark cave in my mind. I still have imaginary friends, and companions, and protectors in my head. It is all here for your inspection of me. Take as you wish or to understand. I thought that since everyone that I gave monies to maybe they would come back and be my friend. I helped them in need, what about me? My Grandma and Grandpa always said to me going to church does not make you a christen anymore than flushing a toilet makes you a plummer. I am exploding in hate from with in the bowels of my soul. The parts of me inside are on fire all the time. I am absolutely pissed off at the whole world for no help. I don't want justice I want to drag both behind my jeep from new york to California non-stop. both being naked belly down on the road. I have no love in my heart or my mind. Just hate. I have been worshiping satan. I only want revenge all the time. My Father took the easy way out he died. Stupid people say don't think about it, and it will go away. How brain dead is that? I have had people judge and slam me, they have no clue the monster that lives in me 24-7. I had a person tell me what did you do to deserve it. I beat the hell out of this person, I was 15 and got sent home from school for 5 days. I have out burst and in bursts of uncontrollable anger. Sometimes I scare myself. I can't let my anger go too long. I tried to fix me with no help, it failed. Everyone was always too late, too little, and always not enough. I am sensitive more than I should be. I try to get to know someone anyone and get hurt along the way. I can't do like other people do. I want a friend to care about me and love me. To honor and be accepted by others. To reflect and to choose however I wanted to choose to trust that person. I thought that when I had a job if I bought things for people they would be my friend. I am several years behind a regular class room children. I raised two beautiful children, and my son is 6 months behind the regular class room children. I smothered them with love. Now is my time to heal, and my husband, son, daughter, and son-in-law told me to do what I need. Sometimes I have problems with making love to my husband. I zone out and start crying and shaking. I sometimes can't have relations with my husband. I went to my doctor 4 to 6 weeks after my Father and his best friend raped, and sodmized me. I told the doctor that I had an boyfriend, but at that time I wasn't dating my future husband. My Father told me to lie. After that before I met my future husband I slepted with everybody, and anyone I didn't care anymore. Everyone around here assumes I was just loose and no good. They didn't want to see. They couldn't see the forest for the trees. I didn't have any confidence or self respect for me or anyone, or anything else. I just wanted all the drugs I could get. All of you stole more than my childhood. I can't trust anyone or even myself. All of you destroyed me, and just wanted me for your own entertainment. This book is it. I always did things different than everyone. My choices were made for me. My experiences have led me to all of you to read, look, and change your point of views. Would I be here sharing my life, my story, my book, and my being. Sometimes I think of going to Kodiak Island and getting it over with, me living. I will never hurt anyone because we all are on our way to being a victem. I was kept under my Father and Mother's thumb. People being mad at me was my biggest worry. I always looked for a change for someone to do the right thing. To help me. I was hurt all the time. I tried so hard to get it to stop. I was ignored by family, teachers, counselors, and assistant princepal. I suffered all the time. If it hadn't been for drugs, sex, and drinking I wouldn't have survived. I never got any justice, or my day in court. I just wanted to be heard and understood. My Father loved to humitated me all the time, and use me for his sex toy. He had a demeaning abusive way with me to do what he wanted. I loved to hate him, wanted to kill him in various ways. He was very good at being manipulating me into doing destructive sexual behavior things with him. He always said that it was my fault. He was selfish because he had to have steak and eat it in front of us, while we ate hot dogs, chips, hamburgers, and other junk food. We had to go around and collect soda bottles to take to the store for money so we could get a hamburger. I trusted him and he took everything that was good and pure. No one saw what a monster he was inside or behind closed doors. I am still emotionally devastated, and wanting to fill that hole left deep inside of me and my soul, and heart. I had to exact a cloud of deception so I could avoid any problems. I was so afraid my grandparents would find out. I am very evasive to keep people from seeing all the shame and pain. I try to refuse people from getting too close. I have a problem with my body because I have put on so much weight. I was always told I have a sexy body growing up and that became a big problem it made me so vain. My Mother would tell me to sit at the big window of my Father's and Mother's restaurant and watch how people walk and told to look at their butts. My Mother would say look at that big butt. My Mother would say look how they walk funny what a funny looking butt that one has, look that one has dimples or their butt. This made me feel very uncomfortable. Sometimes I just wanted to hurt someone, anyone. My parents were dysfunctionally crazy. I am amazed by people who think it is something that can be forgotten just by not thinking of it. My subconscious mind works over time to torture me when I sleep, I have horrible nightmares and real life dreams. I had a dream about a shark biting off both of my legs, and I woke up and could feel the warm blood, I threw back the covers to see if my legs were gone. My Mother would get this crazed look in her eyes, and say things that didn't make any sense at all. All my Father could do is get drunk, and use me for his own needs and wants. My Mother would say now it is resolved you will be with your Father when he wants. My Mother would say she's going to be gone now you go and get in the bed with your Father and pleasure him and his needs, don't resist. My Mother told me it is time I knew what to do while she is gone. My Mother said that she fixed it is all over, no more talk. My Mother said adjusting your mind, to be good with my Father would take up where she left off, now she can have me having a wonderful sex life with my Father made her happy. My Mother said before to me I just didn't know how to make my father happy. My Father wanted my Mother to train me so we could both serve him. My Father wanted me for his own pleasure. My Mother would say to my Father what's going to happen now that they are gone but me. To me being furious was a way of life for me. Everyone that could of helped me should have but I wanted to kill my parents a thousand times a day everyday of my life. I was very much promiscuous, and used every drug I could to erase my brain and memory, which it didn't work. I tried to destroy all my problems and avoid everything I didn't want to remember. I wanted the doctors to take a lazer to burn my memories away. Now I would rather masturbate then have sex. Now I have a real and healthy realationship. I have problems with being overly sexual preversional and having strong thoughts of suicide. I listen to rock and roll to escape for an hour or two. My Mother and Father were selfish, selfcentered, unloving, and emotionally abusive. They treated me like I was to blame, and the plague in their lives, because they told me all of this was my fault. They never took or had any adult responsibilities to my needs or well being. My choices were taken and they made my life for me, and my life was very negative. I have no clue what is right and what is just and what is good or bad or what is sincere. My rage was so sweet because it was for me, and I could swallow it and felt good inside. I will never heal or forget. I want and need front roll seat in hell, sitting beside satan. My Father said to me I was his sweet hot mellon girl for him. He told me they were so pink ripe and juicy. My Father said he is a man and needs to show me his love. My Father told me he is always ready and hard at anytime. My Father said that I need to ask for more when I am with him. My Father wants me too lay on the bed with my legs spread open and pulled back. My Father said how special I was. My Father wanted me to stand over him, and he would finger me. My Father wanted to see me dry hump his leg. He would laugh and squeeze my bottom. My Father told me that I was his. My father said he liked looking at me in the mirrow, so he could put his thing between my legs. My Father would hold me so tight that he would leave big bruises on my sides of my bottom, and thighs. My Mother always said she was suppose to be something better than to have children. She always wanted attention from everyone, and anyone to forget she had children. She would tell my Father that now I am ungrateful, spoiled brat. The aggression line had been moved. My Father's breath was so foul, when he would tongue kiss me I would gag, he would get mad and slap me. He almost never brushed or used mouth wash. Then he said he was going to teach me a lesson. He pushed me down, I went to my knees, My Father was forcing his thing in my mouth, holding my neck tight and hard. My Father telling me to get better balance for me to put my hands on his bottom on each side. I would choke on it then gag on the white stuff. My Father said to me take your finger and put it in my asshole, then take your other finger and rub my balls real soft. I try to get away it's making me sick. My Father told me he wanted to put his hard thing in my ass. My Father said that I am his sweet soft pink mellons juice. I was so small, weak, and frail I couldn't fight you off. The things you said and did I to this day don't understand. I begged, and pleaded for you to stop you laughed, and hurt me anyway. Your best friend always told you that I was better than any other girl, and I was special girl. Both of you would brag about how tight I was when both of you were finished. And I was prettier than any other girl in the whole wide world. You told me when you were finished that I needed more training and discipline, and that is why you said I made you hurt me. I wasn't smart enough that is why you have a need to show me what happens to little ungrateful bratts when I don't try enough to make you happy. All the terrible things that you and your friend put me threw, and the bruises on my thighs. scar my life, reason, innocence. It was all about you and your friend needs no matter the results of destroying your daughter. I think that if I jump off a bridge in the west, maybe there would be a shark in the ocean it would be big enough to swallow me whole. There is nothing bad enough to have you feel or felt like I did and still do. All the pain, hurt, saddness, and the many times I struggled with killing myself can never heal or help me forgive or forget my nightmares I have even now, tomorrow, and forever in my mind. The damage that you inflected on me and in my mind can not be erased, and you couldn't begin to understand, or care to or want to take the time. Every morning, noon, and night I see you as a bottom feeding creature in my mind and dreams waking me up with screams, shaking, crying, and holding my husband crying all of my soul out to god. The hand, house shoe, razor strap, and belt that you hit me with all it did is cause me to hate you much more. All the times my Mother wrote notes that were lies to the schools, spoke volumes about both of your non-parenting growing up. My cries of pain, asking for you please stop, to make you stop hurting me all the times telling you it hurts please leave me alone. Or saying to my Mother she just needs more training. All I have is terror, confusion, and painful memories. I go day by day wishing and hoping, trying to forget and move forward, I just wait and wait. I can't do it. My

Father and his best friend, and the ex-boy friend I dated none of you three gave a good god-damn about me. When the ex-boy friend showed up at one of my friends funeral just to give me a smug smile, and wink at me I just wanted to die. But I was so happy when you died my Father, and I will be so glad when the last two die too. But when you died my Father it didn't help much, but a short lived satisfaction. The message to My Father and his best friend was very clear. You thought I wasn't listening, or looking, or watching for a ray of sun shine, well it happen when I met a saint my husband. You adults should look, listen, because children are watching, learning, and doing as you do not as you say. When I made my first painting in school Mother you told me to throw that stupid retard crap away. I immediately wanted to be adopted by a new family. When I saw you kick a cat just because he was hungry, I just wanted to slap you, and a little of the real creature in you came out. Everybody in my life deserted me, except my grandma, and grandpa. I felt so alone. I know that these feelings will never end. As terrifying as I was recovery wasn't really an issue for me. The man I dated before my husband was no good trash. I think about sometimes how I am so depressed, and think about this everyday, maybe suicide or go rob a bank, and it would be suicide by cop. That is a thought I have had, quick and over in seconds. I feel so used all the time. I look for ways out of this world. I was and I still am in such a state for a long time to come, hurting, emotionally and the physical was real bad too it hurt to sit in school, and I had to be fast with the excuses why I couldn't be active sometimes. The scared feelings of being ashamed were casted so deep, inside I buried them, and didn't want to make eye contact I thought that everyone would see them like I did in the mirrow everyday of my life. My Father and My Mother, and My Father's best friend said to me you had better tell a good enough lie to my teacher in gym class for her to believe it. I was told to say that I fell down the basement steps, so they don't see the bruises when you undress. My Mother said no she can't and will not participate in anyway so the teachers can't see the bruises, because they will ask questions. My Father told my Mother to write a note and call the school. I missed my period and my Father and Mother called my Father's best friend and said she didn't have her period. They were going nuts over it, so they told me to hit myself in the stomach, and fall on the floor on my stomach. All three of them had me do this for a week, because they couldn't trust taking me anywhere that they could trust to keep quite about. I had to fall on the tile floor, that hurt so much. Back then going to the doctor or the hospital that wouldn't do. This insane methods were more of their own insane minds that I had to live with. All I ever wanted is to be safe and have a real family. When I got to go horseback riding I was free for an hour or two just being so happy. I love horses. I hate small places because I was put in a closet by a big woman watching me. Just because I poop my diaper, and wet in it she left me in it all day, and left me in the closet all day. I got an infection in my kidneys, and was blood red down there. I hate being around in a big crowd of people. My fear kicks in when I am in a big crowd, with too many men, or if they are staring at me, and whispering they might be able to sence that I am weak. I am also afraid of being possessed by satan, because I am not living as a catholic. God might think that I am not good enough for him or heaven or his house. Maybe some day I thought that God might send me an angle, or a message to fly me away and talk to me, when he thinks I am good enough to look at. For so long I never thought that anyone would believe me. I felt like I was a coward, loser, and lower than life. I am the plagued with guilt. Feelings of no one would save me or I would die old and alone. Just bury me in the back yard. I was 7 years old when I was home alone with my Father, he had me get naked and lye on the bed with my legs spread, and he started licking my personal place I didn't know what he was doing, but it made me sick and it felt gross, then I felt sick, mad, and sad. When he would spank me it would turn him on, and he would get hard. He would finish by putting his finger in my personal place, and rub. I tried killing myself more times than I can count. I don't have much of a wanting to live. Sometimes I wish I could fall asleep and die. I have nightmares about demons coming after me. Some bad days of zoning out. Sometimes I catch myself not wanting love, and being cold. This is my struggle is trying to get up, and get busy, and to stay busy, so I don't think, but that doesn't work either. I had to learn how to move forward and over come. To live again. To make sence of my life. Time to tell my experiences. To be stronger, or to appear strong. I had no emotions during or after for years until long after. I broke down hard. I felt numb, and thought no one cared, started using every drug in the 70's that I could. Back then I renounced God, and started worshiping satan. When I wasn't high then I would wait until, I could get more drugs, by stealing, everything that I could for money for drugs. I would steal from stores, family, and while I was baby sitting. I had to have the drugs. I didn't want to have time to think, just to be high and feel good. No thinking, no coming down to the real world, I didn't want to remember. When sometimes I wasn't high I was all alone to cry so hard I would vomit, and their was nothing coming up. I didn't eat, just drugs. I was very suicidal, and very homicidal, once when I was coming down off a great acid trip, I loaded our hand gun I stood in-between feeling like this was a calling from God My Father and Mother telling them I would shoot her in the head, then the chest, then shoot him in the side of his head on the right side because he was right-handed, then pick up his hand put the gun in his hand, and have his finger pull the trigger, and shoot me in the shoulder, and the outer leg, so I wouldn't shoot that big artery. I then told them that it would look like a murder suicide. Then wash my hands off with red vinegar, so their would be no gun powder on them, and my involvment would be clear. I also thought that I could get rat poison and put it in their potatoe salad. I stayed alive planning my way out, or killing them too. I was in a bad place in my mind. I wanted to skin them, or make a wish by tying one leg to a fence post and the other to a truck, and that is called making a wish. I had such evil, hatred thoughts inside of me. I think everyday of using a blow torch on his package back then. When I would take a shower I would scrub so hard I would make sores all over me. I had a growing distance with all who didn't think like I did, or listen to what I said. I wanted to kill all the men in the world as I knew it. I was so delusional, and withdrawn, the pressure was going in the red zone. I know I have fought hard and long to get better, and where I am at. It has been a long road. Others that have been in my shoes and have gone threw similar lives like mine. There has been people that have walked in my shoes, that have forgiven their parents, no way I am not there yet, and don't know if I ever will. That fact will never change, I can't find it in my heart to see through all the hate. When I look in the mirrow I see my Mother and Father and his best friend looking back at me, and I am disgusted at what I see. I fought everyday of my life just to move forward one step at a time, then two or three steps back. And the place I slepted it was never a home, just a building. A lot of people have been threw the same hell, and trials and tribulations, and have never had love in their lives like me. I couldn't trust or have commitment that was getting too close to me. Love was too much of anyone to ask. I couldn't open up my heart or me it and I were already dead and dying. I would want to hide everyday. I didn't want to see the all the negative picture of life because it was right in front of me. My Father and Mother told me that all I ever did was embraced the laziness of life to them I could never get anything right. They both never cared to help me or tried to help me, just use me. I didn't have someone to show how to make the right choices years ago. Money was their importance goal not being parents. We were tax right offs that is all. Every opportunity they got both of them refused and push everything aside but money. With the results of how much money they were getting back, they both were happy just having all that money. So I learn by example, not to follow anything the both of you did or said, and Father's best friend will some day have to answer to his crimes. When you Father sent me away to be with your friend for him to do what he wanted, you my Father were killing me on the inside. When you would have good food to eat you didn't care what we ate. When I would leave church you would cuss and yell and threaten, I never understood. I learned threw the years to first trust me then try to trust god on my own terms, and on my own. And on that rare occurrence when a meal was made to impress your Mom, Mother by your wife Father. We would get to have vegetables, and other good food. I took care of my own meals, got ready for school, I walked when you Mother were just too lazy to get up to take me, I walked all the way across town, which was 13 city blocks, when I was in grade school. You my Mother were suppose to see about my home work and study with me, so that I could have gotten out of special ed. Most of the time was spent by gathering up soda bottles to take to the store for money to go get a hamburger. The both of you only helped your selves, and only thought of your needs, didn't care the damage that was done. You would dirty up the house after I would clean all day long, saying that I need to be in the back of the bus like the nigger I was. I didn't know what responsibilities were until I watched other people out in the work field. When I would cry you would say stop that blubbering you cry baby, toughen-up. I know that I never wanted to be like you. I learned most of the lessons I went threw you made a mess of me. I have never been able to be or been productive or never believed in me. I tried to send letters out for help but my Father would get them out of the mail box, and open them tear them up, and cuss at me, and beat me until I promised to never to write another letter. My cries of to keep on trying always failed. I tried one thing after another to be saved. Perhaps, the truth was too much to ask for me. I would value everyone's opinion at this point, to know what I have gone threw. I have had difficulties to overcome my fears, wants, to be loved, excepted, and to maybe find that one true friend. I never favored anyone I never had anyone to favor. everyone said that I had an attitude. That's because they couldn't really see me. Maybe it will be sorted out I don't know about those things, I just want a friend to listen, and have fun. I never had anyone to defend me or my words, or actions. What are actions, I was always left in the dust of everybody else, in the shadows, of life hiding in plain sight. I don't involve myself with people or issues that get to close to their problems, I run and hide. People would push my buttons, and when they saw me getting mad it would turn them on to doing it more and more, just to have fun with me. I just wanted to be left alone in my own little world. I got tired of being the subject of their own sick pleasure. My father was a alcoholic, he would give himself his insulin shot then drink beer with jack daniels in it Both of your thoughts were wrong and your acts and doings were very wrong. My life is over and I will never be what I wanted or could have been. I am very distant, and angry. I was responsible enough to survive. I went threw the emotions day by day. Do to lack of love, kindness, and perspectiveness I don't know how to act in a big crowd of people. I should have a picture of what I am overcoming. Sometimes I just zone-out to escape. Inspite of everything I have challenges to overcome. I needed to have hate and anger as friends. My Father and Mother were the image in the mirror of their gods problems to deal with appropriately. That is what was their answer to everything was let god feed you and see to your needs. The only time that it was different was in the public eye. They never cared about anything or anyone but by using me and destroying everything in me good. I don't know what morals are or anything like that. I don't know what it means to be moral, I never had anyone who cared enough to show me or teach me the right things to do or think, speak, and to be moral, what ever that is? I watched but I don't know what I was supposed to see or think. My Father and Mother were mentally sick, and this passed down mental illness to me. That was a huge aspect of me and my life as I knew it. It's not so black and white, there is a lot of gray. I was told I wasn't even good enough to be around other related families because I was special ed, I wet the bed, and I was retarted, and a disgraceful little pig. They would call me bb boobless blimp while I was getting older. My Father and Mother said that they had a valid point, because they both were the brightest, sensible, and always had the right observation on everything that was important. They would tell everyone that didn't agree with them that they were wrong and they overreacted. Both of my parents were looking threw rose colored glasses, while the rest of the world saw the real world. I have no conifidence. There are some that think woman deserve to be raped. I know I didn't. The sodomy was just as bad, but it did hurt much more. My Father would beat me if I didn't do good in bed, he would beat me furiously, by hitting me where you can't see. One day my Mother was home alone with me. My Father was with his friends. My Mother wanted to sleep so she locked me out of the house. I couldn't go to my grandpa or grandma's house they were out of town. My Mother told me she wanted to sleep. I was out side from 10:00am on a Sunday morning until 10:00pm that night.Whole day I went to my friends house. I went walking around, then I sat out on a curb, until my friends came out to play again. Then at 9:00pm they had to go inside, they told me see you tomorrow. I went and sat on the porch of the house until My Mother unlocked the door. I didn't have anything to drink, eat, and I had to go to the neighbors house to go to the bathroom. I knew better than to say one word, and I didn't dare tell them anything at all. After being outside in 90 to 95 degrees, and the humidity was 98 degrees, I was sick, tired, and light-headed, and vomiting. I was gaging for something to drink. My Mother said to me while rolling her eyes stop it's not like you are going to die, or like you have been in a desert. I still see the house where this all happened. The rage I have is so deep. I went to church but didn't get anything out of it. Then I met a bad boy before my husband, dated him when I was 12 years old until I was 15 and a half years old. He was an excon. He was so dangerous, crazy like a fox. Before my Father and his best friend raped and sodomize me. I begged this excon to help me, get away two weeks before the rape and sodomy happen. I ask why all the

time couldn't someone anyone be there for me? I guess
that I wasn't worth saving. The people who are supposed
to protect us while they are being paid are as crooked
as a dogs hind leg. How many sticks of dynamite do I
need to wake people up, to the reality of this trama, and
damage that this causes. My sister who is 3 years older
than me used a rubber knife to stab on the shower
curtain, while I was taking a shower. It scared me so
bad I peed in the shower. Everyone else was laughing
about it. My freedom was someone elses words not
mine. I was too afraid to begin to trust and open up.
Something inside of me was screaming out to get help.
To fine someone to do something, for them to get up
get out, and get moving in my direction. When I was
in high school I was one of many people teased,
tormented, and bullied threw out for 4 long agonizing
years. I long ago lost the person who I wanted to be, or
was supposed to be. I wanted to be a horse jocky. Win

the triple crown more times than anybody ever did. I know a lot of people would laugh at this. I love pink roses, instead of red roses for wining. Or anything in pink. I was and I am on a rescue mission to save me. Of course about two weeks went by and I was hoping for a miracle, but that never happen for me or to me to deal with all of my troubles. I see so many people where I grew up that didn't care about anything or anybody but them selves. Everyday I walk my own death roll mile. Once I was with my Father and the pipes in the bathrooms of the business that they owned the faucets were left on all day, that night the water froze, and I fell down 27 steps, and hurt my back so bad that I couldn't even walk. My Father and Mother never took me to a doctor, or the emergency room. It took me two weeks for the pain to go away. I told them that I was hurting so bad. They both said take over the counter pain pills. This happen in 1973, when they got the business back because the man they sold it to couldn't make a go of it. My way of life, and my life style, and my feelings, are important to me. Healing is not in my future, and never will be. Basically I was never in a real prison, but I had not one but two Wardens. I always felt like they would and they did make my life of living in a prison cell because they did put me in the hole of their own making. I didn't have people who were faithful around me. I am not one to show love, or want love. And I am not a person to be at ease. I am going to be easy to be evasive, very stand-off kind of a woman. I have a large thing with trust. I keep people at a 10 foot medium. I went to the local drive inn with this boy in school and I said no and he raped me too, before that night I was abused by him. He would kick me in the back, and knock me down. Scraped my knees, and elbows on the gravel in front of my house. I was molested by another neighborhood boy, when I cared for his brothers and sisters, 10 children in all. Another boy told me his sister wanted me to watch her daughter. I went their he told me she would be right back soon, that was a lie. His niece wasn't even their, he grabbed me and slapped me pulled me in a bedroom, and raped me 3 times. I was at a race track and these two guys were saying to each other you lick her boobs, I'll lick her pussy. Then they said we might get a taste of pussy, and give her a taste of our dicks. Then the race track security saw them with another girl in the front stand having sex in front of everyone watching the race. The security guards made them leave.

POEMS

Edgar Allan Poe - A Dream Within A Dream

Take this kiss upon the brow!
And, in parting from you now,
Thus much let me avow--
You are not wrong, who deem
That my days have been a dream;
Yet if hope has flown away
In a night, or in a day,
In a vision, or in none,
Is it therefore the less *gone?*
All that we see or seem
Is but a dream within a dream.

I stand amid the roar
Of a surf-tormented shore,
And I hold within my hand
Grains of the golden sand--
How few! yet how they creep
Through my fingers to the deep,
While I weep--while I weep!
O God! can I not grasp
Them with a tighter clasp?
O God! can I not save
One from the pitiless wave?
Is *all* that we see or seem
But a dream within a dream?

Oliver Wendell Holmes - A Parody on "A Psalm of Life"

Life is real, life is earnest,
And the shell is not its pen –
"Egg thou art, and egg remainest"
Was not spoken of the hen.

Art is long and Time is fleeting,
Be our bills then sharpened well,
And not like muffled drums be beating
On the inside of the shell.

In the world's broad field of battle,
In the great barnyard of life,
Be not like those lazy cattle!
Be a rooster in the strife!

Lives of roosters all remind us,
We can make our lives sublime,
And when roasted, leave behind us,
Hen tracks on the sands of time.

Hen tracks that perhaps another
Chicken drooping in the rain,
Some forlorn and henpecked brother,
When he sees, shall crow again.

Ella Wheeler Wilcox - A Song Of Life

In the rapture of life and of living,
I lift up my head and rejoice,
And I thank the great Giver for giving
The soul of my gladness a voice.
In the glow of the glorious weather,
In the sweet-scented, sensuous air,
My burdens seem light as a feather –
They are nothing to bear.

In the strength and the glory of power,
In the pride and the pleasure of wealth
(For who dares dispute me my dower
Of talents and youth-time and health?) ,
I can laugh at the world and its sages –
I am greater than seers who are sad,
For he is most wise in all ages
Who knows how to be glad.

I lift up my eyes to Apollo,
The god of the beautiful days,
And my spirit soars off like a swallow,
And is lost in the light of its rays.
Are tou troubled and sad? I beseech you
Come out of the shadows of strife –
Come out in the sun while I teach you
The secret of life.

Auna Raunea

Come out of the world – come above it –
Up over its crosses and graves,
Though the green earth is fair and I love it,
We must love it as masters, not slaves.
Come up where the dust never rises –
But only the perfume of flowers –
And your life shall be glad with surprises
Of beautiful hours.
Come up where the rare golden wine is
Apollo distills in my sight,
And your life shall be happy as mine is,
And as full of delight.

Ella Wheeler Wilcox - All Roads That Lead To God Are Good

All roads that lead to God are good.
What matters it, your faith, or mine?
Both centre at the goal divine
Of love's eternal Brotherhood.

The kindly life in house or street –
The life of prayer and mystic rite –
The student's search for truth and light –
These paths at one great Junction meet.

Before the oldest book was writ,
Full many a prehistoric soul
Arrived at this unchanging goal,
Through changeless Love, that leads to it.

What matters that one found his Christ
In rising sun, or burning fire?
In faith within him did not tire,
His longing for the Truth sufficed.

Before our modern hell was brought
To edify the modern world,
Full many a hate-filled soul was hurled
In lakes of fire by its own thought.

A thousand creeds have come and gone,
But what is that to you or me?
Creeds are but branches of a tree –
The root of love lives on and on.

Though branch by branch proved withered wood,
The root is warm with precious wine.
Then keep your faith, and leave me mine –
All roads that lead to God are good.

Alan Seeger - All That's Not Love . . .

All that's not love is the dearth of my days,
The leaves of the volume with rubric unwrit,
The temple in times without prayer, without praise,
The altar unset and the candle unlit.

Let me survive not the lovable sway
Of early desire, nor see when it goes
The courts of Life's abbey in ivied decay,
Whence sometime sweet anthems and incense arose.

The delicate hues of its sevenfold rings
The rainbow outlives not; their yellow and blue
The butterfly sees not dissolve from his wings,
But even with their beauty life fades from them too.

No more would I linger past Love's ardent bounds
Nor live for aught else but the joy that it craves,
That, burden and essence of all that surrounds,
Is the song in the wind and the smile on the waves.

Edgar Allan Poe - Alone

From childhood's hour I have not been
As others were; I have not seen
As others saw; I could not bring
My passions from a common spring.
From the same source I have not taken
My sorrow; I could not awaken
My heart to joy at the same tone;
And all I loved, I loved alone.
Then- in my childhood, in the dawn
Of a most stormy life- was drawn
From every depth of good and ill
The mystery which binds me still:
From the torrent, or the fountain,
From the red cliff of the mountain,
From the sun that round me rolled
In its autumn tint of gold,
From the lightning in the sky
As it passed me flying by,
From the thunder and the storm,
And the cloud that took the form
(When the rest of Heaven was blue)
Of a demon in my view.

Ella Wheeler Wilcox - Ambition's Trail

If all the end of this continuous striving
Were simply to attain,
How poor would seem the planning and contriving
The endless urging and the hurried driving
Of body, heart and brain!

But ever in the wake of true achieving,
There shine this glowing trail –
Some other soul will be spurred on, conceiving,
New strength and hope, in its own power believing,
Because thou didst not fail.

Not thine alone the glory, nor the sorrow,
If thou doth miss the goal,
Undreamed of lives in many a far to-morrow
From thee their weakness or their force shall borrow –
On, on, ambitious soul.

Ella Wheeler Wilcox - An Inspiration

However the battle is ended,
Though proudly the victor comes
With fluttering flags and prancing nags
And echoing roll of drums.
Still truth proclaims this motto,
In letters of living light, -
No Question is ever settled,
Until it is settled right.

Though the heel of the strong oppressor
May grind the weak to dust,
And the voices of fame with one acclaim
May call him great and just,
Let those who applaud take warning,
And keep this motto in sight, -
No question is ever settled
Until it is settled right.

Let those who have failed take courage;
Tho' the enemy seems to have won,
Tho' his ranks are strong, if he be in the wrong
The battle is not yet done;
For, as sure as the morning follows
The darkest hour of the night,
No question is ever settled
Until it is settled right.

O man bowed down with labor!
O woman, young, yet old!
O heart oppressed in the toiler's breast
And crushed by the power of gold!
Keep on with your weary battle
Against triumphant might;
No question is ever settled
Until it is settled right.

Ella Wheeler Wilcox - Answered Prayers

I prayed for riches, and achieved success;
All that I touched turned into gold. Alas!
My cares were greater and my peace was less,
When that wish came to pass.

I prayed for glory, and I heard my name
Sung by sweet children and by hoary men.
But ah! the hurts – the hurts that come with fame.
I was not happy then.

I prayed for Love, and had my heart's desire.
Through quivering heart and body, and through brain,
There swept the flame of its devouring fire,
And but the scars remain.

I prayed for a contented mind. At length
Great light upon my darkened spirit burst.
Great peace fell on me also, and great strength –
Oh, had that prayer been first!

Joyce Kilmer - Apology

(For Eleanor Rogers Cox)

For blows on the fort of evil
That never shows a breach,
For terrible life-long races
To a goal no foot can reach,
For reckless leaps into darkness
With hands outstretched to a star,
There is jubilation in Heaven
Where the great dead poets are.
There is joy over disappointment
And delight in hopes that were vain.
Each poet is glad there was no cure
To stop his lonely pain.
For nothing keeps a poet
In his high singing mood
Like unappeasable hunger
For unattainable food.
So fools are glad of the folly
That made them weep and sing,
And Keats is thankful for Fanny Brawne
And Drummond for his king.
They know that on flinty sorrow
And failure and desire

Auna Raunea

The steel of their souls was hammered
To bring forth the lyric fire.
Lord Byron and Shelley and Plunkett,
McDonough and Hunt and Pearse
See now why their hatred of tyrants
Was so insistently fierce.
Is Freedom only a Will-o'-the-wisp
To cheat a poet's eye?
Be it phantom or fact, it's a noble cause
In which to sing and to die!
So not for the Rainbow taken
And the magical White Bird snared
The poets sing grateful carols
In the place to which they have fared;
But for their lifetime's passion,
The quest that was fruitless and long,
They chorus their loud thanksgiving
To the thorn-crowned Master of Song.

Ella Wheeler Wilcox - As You Go Through Life

Don't look for the flaws as you go through life;
And even when you find them,
It is wise and kind to be somewhat blind
And look for the virtue behind them.
For the cloudiest night has a hint of light
Somewhere in its shadows hiding;
It is better by far to hunt for a star,
Than the spots on the sun abiding.

The current of life runs ever away
To the bosom of God's great ocean.
Don't set your force 'gainst the river's course
And think to alter its motion.
Don't waste a curse on the universe –
Remember it lived before you.
Don't butt at the storm with your puny form,
But bend and let it go o'er you.

The world will never adjust itself
To suit your whims to the letter.
Some things must go wrong your whole life long,
And the sooner you know it the better.
It is folly to fight with the Infinite,
And go under at last in the wrestle;
The wiser man shapes into God's plan
As water shapes into a vessel.

Ella Wheeler Wilcox - Be Not Weary

Sometimes, when I am toil-worn and aweary,
And tired out with working long and well,
And earth is dark, and skies above are dreary,
And heart and soul are all too sick to tell,
These words have come to me like angel fingers
Pressing the spirit's eyelids down in sleep,
'Oh let us not be weary in well doing,
For in due season we shall surely reap.'

Oh, blessed promise! When I seem to hear it,
Whispered by angel voices on the air,
It breathes new life and courage to my spirit,
And gives me strength to suffer and forbear.
And I can wait most patiently for harvest,
And cast my seeds, nor ever faint, nor weep,
If I know surely that my work availeth,
And in God's season, I at last shall reap.

When mind and body were borne down completely,
And I have thought my efforts were all in vain,
These words have come to me so softly, sweetly,
And whispered hope, and urged me on again.
And though my labour seems all unavailing,
And all my striving fruitless, yet the Lord
Doth treasure up each little seed I scatter,
And sometime, sometime, I shall reap the reward.

Ella Wheeler Wilcox - Begin The Day

Begin each morning with a talk to God,
And ask for your divine inheritance
Of usefulness, contentment, and success.
Resign all fear, all doubt, and all despair.
The stars doubt not, and they are undismayed,
Though whirled through space for countless centuries,
And told not why or wherefore: and the sea
With everlasting ebb and flow obeys,
And leaves the purpose with the unseen Cause.
The star sheds its radiance on a million worlds,
The sea is prodigal with waves, and yet
No lustre from the star is lost, and not
One dropp missing from the ocean tides.
Oh! brother to the star and sea, know all
God's opulence is held in trust for those
Who wait serenely and who work in faith.

Ella Wheeler Wilcox - Bird Of Hope

Soar not too high, O bird of Hope!
Because the skies are fair;
The tempest may come on apace
And overcome thee there.

When far above the mountain tops
Thou soarest, over all –
If, then, the storm should press thee back,
How great would be thy fall!

And thou wouldst lie here at my feet,
A poor and lifeless thing, -
A torn and bleeding birdling,
With limp and broken wing.

Sing not too loud, O bird of Hope!
Because the day is bright;
The sunshine cannot always last –
The morn precedes the night.

And if thy song is of the day,
Then when the day grows dim,
Forlorn and voiceless thou wouldst sit
Among the shadows grim.

Oh! I would have thee soar and sing,
But not too high, or loud,
Remembering that day meets night –
The brilliant sun the cloud.

Oliver Wendell Holmes - Contentment
"Man wants but little here below."

LITTLE I ask; my wants are few;
I only wish a hut of stone,
(A very plain brown stone will do,)
That I may call my own;
And close at hand is such a one,
In yonder street that fronts the sun.

Plain food is quite enough for me;
Three courses are as good as ten;--
If Nature can subsist on three,
Thank Heaven for three. Amen!
I always thought cold victual nice;--
My choice would be vanilla-ice.

I care not much for gold or land;--
Give me a mortgage here and there,--
Some good bank-stock, some note of hand,
Or trifling railroad share,--
I only ask that Fortune send
A little more than I shall spend.

Honors are silly toys, I know,
And titles are but empty names;
I would, perhaps, be Plenipo,--
But only near St. James;
I'm very sure I should not care
To fill our Gubernator's chair.

Auna Raunea

Jewels are baubles; 't is a sin
To care for such unfruitful things;--
One good-sized diamond in a pin,--
Some, not so large, in rings,--
A ruby, and a pearl, or so,
Will do for me;--I laugh at show.

My dame should dress in cheap attire;
(Good, heavy silks are never dear;) -
I own perhaps I might desire
Some shawls of true Cashmere,--
Some marrowy crapes of China silk,
Like wrinkled skins on scalded milk.

I would not have the horse I drive
So fast that folks must stop and stare;
An easy gait--two forty-five--
Suits me; I do not care;--
Perhaps, for just a single spurt,
Some seconds less would do no hurt.

Of pictures, I should like to own
Titians aud Raphaels three or four,--
I love so much their style and tone,
One Turner, and no more,
(A landscape,--foreground golden dirt,--
The sunshine painted with a squirt.)

Of books but few,--some fifty score
For daily use, and bound for wear;
The rest upon an upper floor;--
Some little luxury there
Of red morocco's gilded gleam
And vellum rich as country cream.

Busts, cameos, gems,--such things as these,
Which others often show for pride,
I value for their power to please,
And selfish churls deride;--

One Stradivarius, I confess,
Two Meerschaums, I would fain possess.

Wealth's wasteful tricks I will not learn,
Nor ape the glittering upstart fool;--
Shall not carved tables serve my turn,
But all must be of buhl?
Give grasping pomp its double share,--
I ask but one recumbent chair.

Thus humble let me live and die,
Nor long for Midas' golden touch;
If Heaven more generous gifts deny,
I shall not miss them much,--
Too grateful for the blessing lent
Of simple tastes and mind content!

Ella Wheeler Wilcox - Christ Crucified

Now ere I slept, my prayer had been that I might see my way
To do the will of Christ, our Lord and Master, day by day;
And with this prayer upon my lips, I knew not that I dreamed,
But suddenly the world of night a pandemonium seemed.
From forest, and from slaughter house, from bull ring, and from stall,
There rose an anguished cry of pain, a loud, appealing call;
As man – the dumb beast's next of kin – with gun, and whip, and knife,
Went pleasure-seeking through the earth, blood-bent on taking life.
From trap, and cage, and house, and zoo, and street, that awful strain
Of tortured creatures rose and swelled the orchestra of pain.
And then methought the gentle Christ appeared to me and spoke:
'I called you, but ye answered not' – and in my fear I woke.

Then next I heard the roar of mills; and moving through the noise,
Like phantoms in an underworld, were little girls and boys.
Their backs were bent, their brows were pale, their eyes were sad and old;
But by the labour of their hands greed added gold to gold.
Again the Presence and the Voice: 'Behold the crimes I see,
As ye have done it unto these, so have ye done to me.'

Again I slept. I seemed to climb a hard, ascending track;
And just behind me laboured one whose patient face was black.
I pitied him; but hour by hour he gained upon the path;
He stood beside me, stood upright – and then I turned in wrath.
'Go back! ' I cried. 'What right have you to walk beside me here?
For you are black, and I am white.' I paused struck dumb with fear.
For lo! the black man was not there, but Christ stood in his place;
And oh! the pain, the pain, the pain that looked from his dear face.

Now when I woke, the air was rife with that sweet, rhythmic din
Which tells the world that Christ has come to save mankind from sin.
And through the open door of church and temple passed a throng,
To worship Him, with bended knee with sermon, and with song.
But over all I heard the cry of hunted, mangled things;
Those creatures which are part of God, though they have hoofs and
wings.

I saw the mill, the mine, and shop, the little slaves of greed;
I heard the strife of race with race, all sprung from one God-seed.
And then I bowed my head in shame, and in contrition cried –
'Lo, after nineteen hundred years, Christ still is crucified.'

Ralph Waldo Emerson - Days

Daughters of Time, the hypocritic Days,
Muffled and dumb like barefoot dervishes,
And marching single in an endless file,
Bring diadems and fagots in their hands.
To each they offer gifts after his will,
Bread, kingdoms, stars, and sky that holds them all.
I, in my pleached garden, watched the pomp,
Forgot my morning wishes, hastily
Took a few herbs and apples, and the Day
Turned and departed silent. I, too late,
Under her solemn fillet saw the scorn.

Edgar Allan Poe - Dreams

Oh! that my young life were a lasting dream!
My spirit not awakening, till the beam
Of an Eternity should bring the morrow.
Yes! tho' that long dream were of hopeless sorrow,
'Twere better than the cold reality
Of waking life, to him whose heart must be,
And hath been still, upon the lovely earth,
A chaos of deep passion, from his birth.
But should it be- that dream eternally
Continuing- as dreams have been to me
In my young boyhood- should it thus be given,
'Twere folly still to hope for higher Heaven.
For I have revell'd, when the sun was bright
I' the summer sky, in dreams of living light
And loveliness,- have left my very heart
In climes of my imagining, apart
From mine own home, with beings that have been
Of mine own thought- what more could I have seen?
'Twas once- and only once- and the wild hour
From my remembrance shall not pass- some power
Or spell had bound me- 'twas the chilly wind
Came o'er me in the night, and left behind
Its image on my spirit- or the moon
Shone on my slumbers in her lofty noon
Too coldly- or the stars- howe'er it was
That dream was as that night-wind- let it pass.

I have been happy, tho' in a dream.
I have been happy- and I love the theme:
Dreams! in their vivid coloring of life,
As in that fleeting, shadowy, misty strife
Of semblance with reality, which brings
To the delirious eye, more lovely things
Of Paradise and Love- and all our own!
Than young Hope in his sunniest hour hath known.

Alan Seeger - Do You Remember Once . . .

Do you remember once, in Paris of glad faces,
The night we wandered off under the third moon's rays
And, leaving far behind bright streets and busy places,
Stood where the Seine flowed down between its quiet quais?

The city's voice was hushed; the placid, lustrous waters
Mirrored the walls across where orange windows burned.
Out of the starry south provoking rumors brought us
Far promise of the spring already northward turned.

And breast drew near to breast, and round its soft desire
My arm uncertain stole and clung there unrepelled.
I thought that nevermore my heart would hover nigher
To the last flower of bliss that Nature's garden held.

There, in your beauty's sweet abandonment to pleasure,
The mute, half-open lips and tender, wondering eyes,
I saw embodied first smile back on me the treasure
Long sought across the seas and back of summer skies.

Dear face, when courted Death shall claim my limbs and find them
Laid in some desert place, alone or where the tides
Of war's tumultuous waves on the wet sands behind them
Leave rifts of gasping life when their red flood subsides,

Out of the past's remote delirious abysses
Shine forth once more as then you shone, -- beloved head,
Laid back in ecstasy between our blinding kisses,
Transfigured with the bliss of being so coveted.

And my sick arms will part, and though hot fever sear it,
My mouth will curve again with the old, tender flame.
And darkness will come down, still finding in my spirit
The dream of your brief love, and on my lips your name.

II

You loved me on that moonlit night long since.
You were my queen and I the charming prince
Elected from a world of mortal men.
You loved me once. . . . What pity was it, then,
You loved not Love. . . . Deep in the emerald west,
Like a returning caravel caressed
By breezes that load all the ambient airs
With clinging fragrance of the bales it bears
From harbors where the caravans come down,
I see over the roof-tops of the town
The new moon back again, but shall not see
The joy that once it had in store for me,
Nor know again the voice upon the stair,
The little studio in the candle-glare,
And all that makes in word and touch and glance
The bliss of the first nights of a romance
When will to love and be beloved casts out
The want to question or the will to doubt.
You loved me once. . . . Under the western seas
The pale moon settles and the Pleiades.
The firelight sinks; outside the night-winds moan --
The hour advances, and I sleep alone.

III

Farewell, dear heart, enough of vain despairing!
If I have erred I plead but one excuse --
The jewel were a lesser joy in wearing
That cost a lesser agony to lose.

I had not bid for beautifuller hours
Had I not found the door so near unsealed,
Nor hoped, had you not filled my arms with flowers,
For that one flower that bloomed too far afield.

Auna Raunea

If I have wept, it was because, forsaken,
I felt perhaps more poignantly than some
The blank eternity from which we waken
And all the blank eternity to come.

And I betrayed how sweet a thing and tender
(In the regret with which my lip was curled)
Seemed in its tragic, momentary splendor
My transit through the beauty of the world.

Edgar Allan Poe - Dreamland

By a route obscure and lonely,
Haunted by ill angels only,
Where an Eidolon, named NIGHT,
On a black throne reigns upright,
I have reached these lands but newly
From an ultimate dim Thule-
From a wild clime that lieth, sublime,
Out of SPACE- out of TIME.

Bottomless vales and boundless floods,
And chasms, and caves, and Titan woods,
With forms that no man can discover
For the tears that drip all over;
Mountains toppling evermore
Into seas without a shore;
Seas that restlessly aspire,
Surging, unto skies of fire;
Lakes that endlessly outspread
Their lone waters- lone and dead,-
Their still waters- still and chilly
With the snows of the lolling lily.

By the lakes that thus outspread
Their lone waters, lone and dead,-
Their sad waters, sad and chilly
With the snows of the lolling lily,-
By the mountains- near the river
Murmuring lowly, murmuring ever,-
By the grey woods,- by the swamp
Where the toad and the newt encamp-
By the dismal tarns and pools
Where dwell the Ghouls,-
By each spot the most unholy-
In each nook most melancholy-
There the traveller meets aghast
Sheeted Memories of the Past-

Auna Raunea

Shrouded forms that start and sigh
As they pass the wanderer by–
White-robed forms of friends long given,
In agony, to the Earth- and Heaven.

For the heart whose woes are legion
'Tis a peaceful, soothing region–
For the spirit that walks in shadow
'Tis- oh, 'tis an Eldorado!
But the traveller, travelling through it,
May not- dare not openly view it!
Never its mysteries are exposed
To the weak human eye unclosed;
So wills its King, who hath forbid
The uplifting of the fringed lid;
And thus the sad Soul that here passes
Beholds it but through darkened glasses.

By a route obscure and lonely,
Haunted by ill angels only,
Where an Eidolon, named NIGHT,
On a black throne reigns upright,
I have wandered home but newly
From this ultimate dim Thule.

Ralph Waldo Emerson - Each And All

Little thinks, in the field, yon red-cloaked clown,
Of thee, from the hill-top looking down;
And the heifer, that lows in the upland farm,
Far-heard, lows not thine ear to charm;
The sexton tolling the bell at noon,
Dreams not that great Napoleon
Stops his horse, and lists with delight,
Whilst his files sweep round yon Alpine height;
Nor knowest thou what argument
Thy life to thy neighbor's creed has lent:
All are needed by each one,
Nothing is fair or good alone.

I thought the sparrow's note from heaven,
Singing at dawn on the alder bough;
I brought him home in his nest at even;—
He sings the song, but it pleases not now;
For I did not bring home the river and sky;
He sang to my ear; they sang to my eye.

The delicate shells lay on the shore;
The bubbles of the latest wave
Fresh pearls to their enamel gave;
And the bellowing of the savage sea
Greeted their safe escape to me;
I wiped away the weeds and foam,
And fetched my sea-born treasures home;
But the poor, unsightly, noisome things
Had left their beauty on the shore
With the sun, and the sand, and the wild uproar.

Auna Raunea

The lover watched his graceful maid
As 'mid the virgin train she strayed,
Nor knew her beauty's best attire
Was woven still by the snow-white quire;
At last she came to his hermitage,
Like the bird from the woodlands to the cage,—
The gay enchantment was undone,
A gentle wife, but fairy none.

Then I said, "I covet Truth;
Beauty is unripe childhood's cheat,—
I leave it behind with the games of youth."
As I spoke, beneath my feet
The ground-pine curled its pretty wreath,
Running over the club-moss burrs;
I inhaled the violet's breath;
Around me stood the oaks and firs;
Pine cones and acorns lay on the ground;
Above me soared the eternal sky,
Full of light and deity;
Again I saw, again I heard,
The rolling river, the morning bird;—
Beauty through my senses stole,
I yielded myself to the perfect whole.

Ralph Waldo Emerson - Eros

The sense of the world is short,
Long and various the report,—
To love and be beloved;
Men and gods have not outlearned it,
And how oft soe'er they've turned it,
'Tis not to be improved.

Edgar Allan Poe - Evening Star

'Twas noontide of summer,
And mid-time of night;
And stars, in their orbits,
Shone pale, thro' the light
Of the brighter, cold moon,
'Mid planets her slaves,
Herself in the Heavens,
Her beam on the waves.
I gazed awhile
On her cold smile;
Too cold- too cold for me-
There pass'd, as a shroud,
A fleecy cloud,
And I turned away to thee,
Proud Evening Star,
In thy glory afar,
And dearer thy beam shall be;
For joy to my heart
Is the proud part
Thou bearest in Heaven at night,
And more I admire
Thy distant fire,
Than that colder, lowly light.

Ralph Waldo Emerson - Fable

The mountain and the squirrel
Had a quarrel,
And the former called the latter, "little prig":
Bun replied,
You are doubtless very big,
But all sorts of things and weather
Must be taken in together
To make up a year,
And a sphere.
And I think it no disgrace
To occupy my place.
If I'm not so large as you,
You are not so small as I,
And not half so spry:
I'll not deny you make
A very pretty squirrel track;
Talents differ; all is well and wisely put;
If I cannot carry forests on my back,
Neither can you crack a nut.

Ralph Waldo Emerson - Fate

That you are fair or wise is vain,
Or strong, or rich, or generous;
You must have also the untaught strain
That sheds beauty on the rose.
There is a melody born of melody,
Which melts the world into a sea.
Toil could never compass it,
Art its height could never hit,
It came never out of wit,
But a music music-born
Well may Jove and Juno scorn.
Thy beauty, if it lack the fire
Which drives me mad with sweet desire,
What boots it? what the soldier's mail,
Unless he conquer and prevail?
What all the goods thy pride which lift,
If thou pine for another's gift?
Alas! that one is born in blight,
Victim of perpetual slight;—
When thou lookest in his face,
Thy heart saith, Brother! go thy ways!
None shall ask thee what thou doest,
Or care a rush for what thou knowest,
Or listen when thou repliest,
Or remember where thou liest,
Or how thy supper is sodden,—
And another is born
To make the sun forgotten.
Surely he carries a talisman
Under his tongue;

Broad are his shoulders, and strong,
And his eye is scornful,
Threatening, and young.
I hold it of little matter,
Whether your jewel be of pure water,
A rose diamond or a white,—
But whether it dazzle me with light.
I care not how you are drest,
In the coarsest, or in the best,
Nor whether your name is base or brave,
Nor tor the fashion of your behavior,—
But whether you charm me,
Bid my bread feed, and my fire warm me,
And dress up nature in your favor.
One thing is forever good,
That one thing is success,—
Dear to the Eumenides,
And to all the heavenly brood.
Who bides at home, nor looks abroad,
Carries the eagles, and masters the sword.

Oliver Wendell Holmes - The Flower of Liberty

WHAT flower is this that greets the morn,
Its hues from Heaven so freshly born?
With burning star and flaming band
It kindles all the sunset land:
Oh tell us what its name may be,--
Is this the Flower of Liberty?

It is the banner of the free,
The starry Flower of Liberty!

In savage Nature's far abode
Its tender seed our fathers sowed;
The storm-winds rocked its swelling bud,
Its opening leaves were streaked with blood,
Till lo! earth's tyrants shook to see
The full-blown Flower of Liberty!

Then hail the banner of the free,
The starry Flower of Liberty!

Behold its streaming rays unite,
One mingling flood of braided light,--
The red that fires the Southern rose,
With spotless white from Northern snows,
And, spangled o'er its azure, see
The sister Stars of Liberty!

Then hail the banner of the free,
The starry Flower of Liberty!

The blades of heroes fence it round,
Where'er it springs is holy ground;
From tower and dome its glories spread;
It waves where lonely sentries tread;
It makes the land as ocean free,
And plants an empire on the sea!

Then hail the banner of the free,
The starry Flower of Liberty!

Thy sacred leaves, fair Freedom's flower,
Shall ever float on dome and tower,
To all their heavenly colors true,
In blackening frost or crimson dew,--
And God love us as we love thee,
Thrice holy Flower of Liberty!

Then hail the banner of the free,
The starry FLOWER OF LIBERTY!

Ralph Waldo Emerson - Give All To Love

Give all to love;
Obey thy heart;
Friends, kindred, days,
Estate, good fame,
Plans, credit, and the muse;
Nothing refuse.

'Tis a brave master,
Let it have scope,
Follow it utterly,
Hope beyond hope;
High and more high,
It dives into noon,
With wing unspent,
Untold intent;
But 'tis a god,
Knows its own path,
And the outlets of the sky.
'Tis not for the mean,
It requireth courage stout,
Souls above doubt,
Valor unbending;
Such 'twill reward,
They shall return
More than they were,
And ever ascending.

Leave all for love;—
Yet, hear me, yet,
One word more thy heart behoved,
One pulse more of firm endeavor,
Keep thee to-day,
To-morrow, for ever,
Free as an Arab
Of thy beloved.
Cling with life to the maid;
But when the surprise,
Vague shadow of surmise,
Flits across her bosom young
Of a joy apart from thee,
Free be she, fancy-free,
Do not thou detain a hem,
Nor the palest rose she flung
From her summer diadem.

Though thou loved her as thyself,
As a self of purer clay,
Tho' her parting dims the day,
Stealing grace from all alive,
Heartily know,
When half-gods go,
The gods arrive.

Ralph Waldo Emerson - Good-by

Good-by, proud world, I'm going home,
Thou'rt not my friend, and I'm not thine;
Long through thy weary crowds I roam;
A river-ark on the ocean brine,
Long I've been tossed like the driven foam,
But now, proud world, I'm going home.

Good-by to Flattery's fawning face,
To Grandeur, with his wise grimace,
To upstart Wealth's averted eye,
To supple Office low and high,
To crowded halls, to court, and street,
To frozen hearts, and hasting feet,
To those who go, and those who come,
Good-by, proud world, I'm going home.

I'm going to my own hearth-stone
Bosomed in yon green hills, alone,
A secret nook in a pleasant land,
Whose groves the frolic fairies planned;
Where arches green the livelong day
Echo the blackbird's roundelay,
And vulgar feet have never trod
A spot that is sacred to thought and God.

Oh, when I am safe in my sylvan home,
I tread on the pride of Greece and Rome;
And when I am stretched beneath the pines
Where the evening star so holy shines,
I laugh at the lore and the pride of man,
At the sophist schools, and the learned clan;
For what are they all in their high conceit,
When man in the bush with God may meet.

Joyce Kilmer - In Memory

I
Serene and beautiful and very wise,
Most erudite in curious Grecian lore,
You lay and read your learned books, and bore
A weight of unshed tears and silent sighs.
The song within your heart could never rise
Until love bade it spread its wings and soar.
Nor could you look on Beauty's face before
A poet's burning mouth had touched your eyes.
Love is made out of ecstasy and wonder;
Love is a poignant and accustomed pain.
It is a burst of Heaven-shaking thunder;
It is a linnet's fluting after rain.
Love's voice is through your song; above and under
And in each note to echo and remain.

II
Because Mankind is glad and brave and young,
Full of gay flames that white and scarlet glow,
All joys and passions that Mankind may know
By you were nobly felt and nobly sung.
Because Mankind's heart every day is wrung
By Fate's wild hands that twist and tear it so,
Therefore you echoed Man's undying woe,
A harp Aeolian on Life's branches hung.
So did the ghosts of toiling children hover
About the piteous portals of your mind;
Your eyes, that looked on glory, could discover
The angry scar to which the world was blind:
And it was grief that made Mankind your lover,
And it was grief that made you love Mankind.

III

Before Christ left the Citadel of Light,
To tread the dreadful way of human birth,
His shadow sometimes fell upon the earth
And those who saw it wept with joy and fright.
"Thou art Apollo, than the sun more bright!"
They cried. "Our music is of little worth,
But thrill our blood with thy creative mirth
Thou god of song, thou lord of lyric might!"
O singing pilgrim! who could love and follow
Your lover Christ, through even love's despair,
You knew within the cypress-darkened hollow
The feet that on the mountain are so fair.
For it was Christ that was your own Apollo,
And thorns were in the laurel on your hair.

Edgar Allan Poe - In the Greenest of our Valleys

I.
In the greenest of our valleys,
By good angels tenanted,
Once fair and stately palace --
Radiant palace --reared its head.
In the monarch Thought's dominion --
It stood there!
Never seraph spread a pinion
Over fabric half so fair.

II.
Banners yellow, glorious, golden,
On its roof did float and flow;
(This --all this --was in the olden
Time long ago)
And every gentle air that dallied,
In that sweet day,
Along the ramparts plumed and pallid,
A winged odour went away.

III.
Wanderers in that happy valley
Through two luminous windows saw
Spirits moving musically
To a lute's well-tuned law,
Round about a throne, where sitting
(Porphyrogene!)
In state his glory well befitting,
The ruler of the realm was seen.

IV.
And all with pearl and ruby glowing
Was the fair palace door,
Through which came flowing, flowing, flowing
And sparkling evermore,
A troop of Echoes whose sweet duty
Was but to sing,
In voices of surpassing beauty,
The wit and wisdom of their king.

V.
But evil things, in robes of sorrow,
Assailed the monarch's high estate;
(Ah, let us mourn, for never morrow
Shall dawn upon him, desolate!)
And, round about his home, the glory
That blushed and bloomed
Is but a dim-remembered story
Of the old time entombed.

VI.
And travellers now within that valley,
Through the red-litten windows, see
Vast forms that move fantastically
To a discordant melody;
While, like a rapid ghastly river,
Through the pale door,
A hideous throng rush out forever,
And laugh --but smile no more.

Ralph Waldo Emerson - Loss And Gain

Virtue runs before the muse
And defies her skill,
She is rapt, and doth refuse
To wait a painter's will.

Star-adoring, occupied,
Virtue cannot bend her,
Just to please a poet's pride,
To parade her splendor.

The bard must be with good intent
No more his, but hers,
Throw away his pen and paint,
Kneel with worshippers.

Then, perchance, a sunny ray
From the heaven of fire,
His lost tools may over-pay,
And better his desire.

Joyce Kilmer - Madness
(For Sara Teasdale)

The lonely farm, the crowded street,
The palace and the slum,
Give welcome to my silent feet
As, bearing gifts, I come.
Last night a beggar crouched alone,
A ragged helpless thing;
I set him on a moonbeam throne --
Today he is a king.
Last night a king in orb and crown
Held court with splendid cheer;
Today he tears his purple gown
And moans and shrieks in fear.
Not iron bars, nor flashing spears,
Not land, nor sky, nor sea,
Nor love's artillery of tears
Can keep mine own from me.
Serene, unchanging, ever fair,
I smile with secret mirth
And in a net of mine own hair
I swing the captive earth.

Ralph Waldo Emerson - Ode To Beauty

Who gave thee, O Beauty!
The keys of this breast,
Too credulous lover
Of blest and unblest?
Say when in lapsed ages
Thee knew I of old;
Or what was the service
For which I was sold?
When first my eyes saw thee,
I found me thy thrall,
By magical drawings,
Sweet tyrant of all!
I drank at thy fountain
False waters of thirst;
Thou intimate stranger,
Thou latest and first!
Thy dangerous glances
Make women of men;
New-born we are melting
Into nature again.
Lavish, lavish promiser,
Nigh persuading gods to err,
Guest of million painted forms
Which in turn thy glory warms,
The frailest leaf, the mossy bark,
The acorn's cup, the raindrop's arc,
The swinging spider's silver line,
The ruby of the drop of wine,
The shining pebble of the pond,
Thou inscribest with a bond
In thy momentary play
Would bankrupt Nature to repay.

Auna Raunea

Ah! what avails it
To hide or to shun
Whom the Infinite One
Hath granted his throne?
The heaven high over
Is the deep's lover,
The sun and sea
Informed by thee,
Before me run,
And draw me on,
Yet fly me still,
As Fate refuses
To me the heart Fate for me chooses,
Is it that my opulent soul
Was mingled from the generous whole,
Sea valleys and the deep of skies
Furnished several supplies,
And the sands whereof I'm made
Draw me to them self-betrayed?
I turn the proud portfolios
Which hold the grand designs
Of Salvator, of Guercino,
And Piranesi's lines.
I hear the lofty Pæans
Of the masters of the shell,
Who heard the starry music,
And recount the numbers well:
Olympian bards who sung
Divine Ideas below,
Which always find us young,
And always keep us so.
Oft in streets or humblest places
I detect far wandered graces,
Which from Eden wide astray
In lowly homes have lost their way.

Thee gliding through the sea of form,
Like the lightning through the storm,
Somewhat not to be possessed,
Somewhat not to be caressed,
No feet so fleet could ever find,
No perfect form could ever bind.
Thou eternal fugitive
Hovering over all that live,
Quick and skilful to inspire
Sweet extravagant desire,
Starry space and lily bell
Filling with thy roseate smell,
Wilt not give the lips to taste
Of the nectar which thou hast.

All that's good and great with thee
Stands in deep conspiracy.
Thou hast bribed the dark and lonely
To report thy features only,
And the cold and purple morning
Itself with thoughts of thee adorning,
The leafy dell, the city mart,
Equal trophies of thine art,
E'en the flowing azure air
Thou hast touched for my despair,
And if I languish into dreams,
Again I meet the ardent beams.
Queen of things! I dare not die
In Being's deeps past ear and eye,
Lest there I find the same deceiver,
And be the sport of Fate forever.
Dread power, but dear! if God thou be,
Unmake me quite, or give thyself to me.

Alan Seeger - I Have A Rendezvous With Death

I have a rendezvous with Death
At some disputed barricade,
When Spring comes back with rustling shade
And apple-blossoms fill the air—
I have a rendezvous with Death
When Spring brings back blue days and fair.

It may be he shall take my hand
And lead me into his dark land
And close my eyes and quench my breath—
It may be I shall pass him still.
I have a rendezvous with Death
On some scarred slope of battered hill
When Spring comes round again this year
And the first meadow-flowers appear.

God knows 'twere better to be deep
Pillowed in silk and scented down,
Where Love throbs out in blissful sleep,
Pulse nigh to pulse, and breath to breath,
Where hushed awakenings are dear...
But I've a rendezvous with Death
At midnight in some flaming town,
When Spring trips north again this year,
And I to my pledged word am true,
I shall not fail that rendezvous.

Joyce Kilmer - Roses
(For Katherine Bregy)

I went to gather roses and twine them in a ring,
For I would make a posy, a posy for the King.
I got an hundred roses, the loveliest there be,
From the white rose vine and the pink rose bush and from the red
rose tree.
But when I took my posy and laid it at His feet
I found He had His roses a million times more sweet.
There was a scarlet blossom upon each foot and hand,
And a great pink rose bloomed from His side for the healing of the
land.
Now of this fair and awful King there is this marvel told,
That He wears a crown of linked thorns instead of one of gold.
Where there are thorns are roses, and I saw a line of red,
A little wreath of roses around His radiant head.
A red rose is His Sacred Heart, a white rose is His face,
And His breath has turned the barren world to a rich and flowery
place.
He is the Rose of Sharon, His gardener am I,
And I shall drink His fragrance in Heaven when I die.

Edgar Allan Poe - Serenade

So sweet the hour, so calm the time,
I feel it more than half a crime,
When Nature sleeps and stars are mute,
To mar the silence ev'n with lute.
At rest on ocean's brilliant dyes
An image of Elysium lies:
Seven Pleiades entranced in Heaven,
Form in the deep another seven:
Endymion nodding from above
Sees in the sea a second love.
Within the valleys dim and brown,
And on the spectral mountain's crown,
The wearied light is dying down,
And earth, and stars, and sea, and sky
Are redolent of sleep, as I
Am redolent of thee and thine
Enthralling love, my Adeline.
But list, O list,- so soft and low
Thy lover's voice tonight shall flow,
That, scarce awake, thy soul shall deem
My words the music of a dream.
Thus, while no single sound too rude
Upon thy slumber shall intrude,
Our thoughts, our souls- O God above!
In every deed shall mingle, love.

Oliver Wendell Holmes - The Silent Melody

"BRING me my broken harp," he said;
"We both are wrecks,-- but as ye will,--
Though all its ringing tones have fled,
Their echoes linger round it still;
It had some golden strings, I know,
But that was long-- how long!-- ago.

"I cannot see its tarnished gold,
I cannot hear its vanished tone,
Scarce can my trembling fingers hold
The pillared frame so long their own;
We both are wrecks,-- awhile ago
It had some silver strings, I know,

"But on them Time too long has played
The solemn strain that knows no change,
And where of old my fingers strayed
The chords they find are new and strange,--
Yes! iron strings,-- I know,-- I know,--
We both are wrecks of long ago.

"We both are wrecks,-- a shattered pair,
Strange to ourselves in time's disguise
What say ye to the lovesick air
That brought the tears from Marian's eyes?
Ay! trust me,-- under breasts of snow
Hearts could be melted long ago!

"Or will ye hear the storm-song's crash
That from his dreams the soldier woke,
And bade him face the lightning flash
When battle's cloud in thunder broke?
Wrecks,-- nought but wrecks!-- the time was when
We two were worth a thousand men!"

Auna Raunea

And so the broken harp they bring
With pitying smiles that none could blame;
Alas there's not a single string
Of all that filled the tarnished frame!
But see! like children overjoyed,
His fingers rambling through the void!

"I clasp thee! Ay . . . mine ancient lyre. . .
Nay, guide my wandering fingers. . . There!
They love to dally with the wire
As Isaac played with Esan's hair. . . .
Hush! ye shall hear the famous tune
That Marina called the Breath of June!"

And so they softly gather round:
Rapt in his tuneful trance he seems:
His fingers move: but not a sound!
A silence like the song of dreams. . . .
"There! ye have heard the air," he cries,
"That brought the tears from Marina's eyes!"

Ah, smile not at his fond conceit,
Nor deem his fancy wrought in vain;
To him the unreal sounds are sweet,--
No discord mars the silent strain
Scored on life's latest, starlit page--
The voiceless melody of age.

Sweet are the lips of all that sing,
When Nature's music breathes unsought,
But never yet could voice or string
So truly shape our tenderest thought
As when by life's decaying fire
Our fingers sweep the stringless lyre!

Ella Wheeler Wilcox - A Song Of Life

In the rapture of life and of living,
I lift up my head and rejoice,
And I thank the great Giver for giving
The soul of my gladness a voice.
In the glow of the glorious weather,
In the sweet-scented, sensuous air,
My burdens seem light as a feather –
They are nothing to bear.

In the strength and the glory of power,
In the pride and the pleasure of wealth
(For who dares dispute me my dower
Of talents and youth-time and health?) ,
I can laugh at the world and its sages –
I am greater than seers who are sad,
For he is most wise in all ages
Who knows how to be glad.

I lift up my eyes to Apollo,
The god of the beautiful days,
And my spirit soars off like a swallow,
And is lost in the light of its rays.
Are tou troubled and sad? I beseech you
Come out of the shadows of strife –
Come out in the sun while I teach you
The secret of life.

Auna Raunea

Come out of the world – come above it –
Up over its crosses and graves,
Though the green earth is fair and I love it,
We must love it as masters, not slaves.
Come up where the dust never rises –
But only the perfume of flowers –
And your life shall be glad with surprises
Of beautiful hours.
Come up where the rare golden wine is
Apollo distills in my sight,
And your life shall be happy as mine is,
And as full of delight.

Oliver Wendell Holmes - Sun and Shadow

As I look from the isle, o'er its billows of green,
To the billows of foam-crested blue,
Yon bark, that afar in the distance is seen,
Half dreaming, my eyes will pursue:
Now dark in the shadow, she scatters the spray
As the chaff in the stroke of the flail;
Now white as the sea-gull, she flies on her way,
The sun gleaming bright on her sail.

Yet her pilot is thinking of dangers to shun,--
Of breakers that whiten and roar;
How little he cares, if in shadow or sun
They see him who gaze from the shore!
He looks to the beacon that looms from the reef,
To the rock that is under his lee,
As he drifts on the blast, like a wind-wafted leaf,
O'er the gulfs of the desolate sea.

Thus drifting afar to the dim-vaulted caves
Where life and its ventures are laid,
The dreamers who gaze while we battle the waves
May see us in sunshine or shade;
Yet true to our course, though the shadows grow dark,
We'll trim our broad sail as before,
And stand by the rudder that governs the bark,
Nor ask how we look from the shore!

Ralph Waldo Emerson - Tact

What boots it, thy virtue,
What profit thy parts,
While one thing thou lackest,
The art of all arts!
The only credentials,
Passport to success,
Opens castle and parlor,—
Address, man, Address.

The maiden in danger
Was saved by the swain,
His stout arm restored her
To Broadway again:

The maid would reward him,—
Gay company come,—
They laugh, she laughs with them,
He is moonstruck and dumb.

This clenches the bargain,
Sails out of the bay,
Gets the vote in the Senate,
Spite of Webster and Clay;

Has for genius no mercy,
For speeches no heed,—
It lurks in the eyebeam,
It leaps to its deed.

Church, tavern, and market,
Bed and board it will sway;
It has no to-morrow,
It ends with to-day.

Ralph Waldo Emerson - The Barberry Bush

The bush that has most briers and bitter fruit,
Wait till the frost has turned its green leaves red,
Its sweetened berries will thy palate suit,
And thou may'st find e'en there a homely bread.
Upon the hills of Salem scattered wide,
Their yellow blossoms gain the eye in Spring;
And straggling e'en upon the turnpike's side,
Their ripened branches to your hand they bring,
I 've plucked them oft in boyhood's early hour,
That then I gave such name, and thought it true;
But now I know that other fruit as sour
Grows on what now thou callest Me and You;
Yet, wilt thou wait the autumn that I see,
Will sweeter taste than these red berries be.

Ralph Waldo Emerson - The Bell

I love thy music, mellow bell,
I love thine iron chime,
To life or death, to heaven or hell,
Which calls the sons of Time.

Thy voice upon the deep
The home-bound sea-boy hails,
It charms his cares to sleep,
It cheers him as he sails.

To house of God and heavenly joys
Thy summons called our sires,
And good men thought thy sacred voice
Disarmed the thunder's fires.

And soon thy music, sad death-bell,
Shall lift its notes once more,
And mix my requiem with the wind
That sweeps my native shore.

Edgar Allan Poe - The Bells

I

Hear the sledges with the bells-
Silver bells!
What a world of merriment their melody foretells!
How they tinkle, tinkle, tinkle,
In the icy air of night!
While the stars that oversprinkle
All the heavens, seem to twinkle
With a crystalline delight;
Keeping time, time, time,
In a sort of Runic rhyme,
To the tintinnabulation that so musically wells
From the bells, bells, bells, bells,
Bells, bells, bells-
From the jingling and the tinkling of the bells.

II

Hear the mellow wedding bells,
Golden bells!
What a world of happiness their harmony foretells!
Through the balmy air of night
How they ring out their delight!
From the molten-golden notes,
And an in tune,
What a liquid ditty floats
To the turtle-dove that listens, while she gloats
On the moon!
Oh, from out the sounding cells,
What a gush of euphony voluminously wells!
How it swells!
How it dwells
On the Future! how it tells
Of the rapture that impels
To the swinging and the ringing

Of the bells, bells, bells,
Of the bells, bells, bells,bells,
Bells, bells, bells-
To the rhyming and the chiming of the bells!

III

Hear the loud alarum bells-
Brazen bells!
What a tale of terror, now, their turbulency tells!
In the startled ear of night
How they scream out their affright!
Too much horrified to speak,
They can only shriek, shriek,
Out of tune,
In a clamorous appealing to the mercy of the fire,
In a mad expostulation with the deaf and frantic fire,
Leaping higher, higher, higher,
With a desperate desire,
And a resolute endeavor,
Now- now to sit or never,
By the side of the pale-faced moon.
Oh, the bells, bells, bells!
What a tale their terror tells
Of Despair!
How they clang, and clash, and roar!
What a horror they outpour
On the bosom of the palpitating air!
Yet the ear it fully knows,
By the twanging,
And the clanging,
How the danger ebbs and flows:
Yet the ear distinctly tells,
In the jangling,
And the wrangling,
How the danger sinks and swells,
By the sinking or the swelling in the anger of the bells-
Of the bells-
Of the bells, bells, bells,bells,

Bells, bells, bells-
In the clamor and the clangor of the bells!

IV

Hear the tolling of the bells-
Iron Bells!
What a world of solemn thought their monody compels!
In the silence of the night,
How we shiver with affright
At the melancholy menace of their tone!
For every sound that floats
From the rust within their throats
Is a groan.
And the people- ah, the people-
They that dwell up in the steeple,
All Alone
And who, tolling, tolling, tolling,
In that muffled monotone,
Feel a glory in so rolling
On the human heart a stone-
They are neither man nor woman-
They are neither brute nor human-
They are Ghouls:
And their king it is who tolls;
And he rolls, rolls, rolls,
Rolls
A paean from the bells!
And his merry bosom swells
With the paean of the bells!
And he dances, and he yells;
Keeping time, time, time,
In a sort of Runic rhyme,
To the paean of the bells-
Of the bells:
Keeping time, time, time,
In a sort of Runic rhyme,
To the throbbing of the bells-
Of the bells, bells, bells-

Auna Raunea

To the sobbing of the bells;
Keeping time, time, time,
As he knells, knells, knells,
In a happy Runic rhyme,
To the rolling of the bells-
Of the bells, bells, bells:
To the tolling of the bells,
Of the bells, bells, bells, bells-
Bells, bells, bells-
To the moaning and the groaning of the bells.

Edgar Allan Poe - The City In The Sea

Lo! Death has reared himself a throne
In a strange city lying alone
Far down within the dim West,
Where the good and the bad and the worst and the best
Have gone to their eternal rest.
There shrines and palaces and towers
(Time-eaten towers that tremble not!)
Resemble nothing that is ours.
Around, by lifting winds forgot,
Resignedly beneath the sky
The melancholy waters lie.

No rays from the holy heaven come down
On the long night-time of that town;
But light from out the lurid sea
Streams up the turrets silently—
Gleams up the pinnacles far and free—
Up domes—up spires—up kingly halls—
Up fanes—up Babylon-like walls—
Up shadowy long-forgotten bowers
Of sculptured ivy and stone flowers—
Up many and many a marvellous shrine
Whose wreathed friezes intertwine
The viol, the violet, and the vine.

Resignedly beneath the sky
The melancholy waters lie.
So blend the turrets and shadows there
That all seem pendulous in air,
While from a proud tower in the town
Death looks gigantically down.

Auna Raunea

There open fanes and gaping graves
Yawn level with the luminous waves;
But not the riches there that lie
In each idol's diamond eye—
Not the gaily-jewelled dead
Tempt the waters from their bed;
For no ripples curl, alas!
Along that wilderness of glass—
No swellings tell that winds may be
Upon some far-off happier sea—
No heavings hint that winds have been
On seas less hideously serene.

But lo, a stir is in the air!
The wave—there is a movement there!
As if the towers had thrust aside,
In slightly sinking, the dull tide—
As if their tops had feebly given
A void within the filmy Heaven.
The waves have now a redder glow—
The hours are breathing faint and low—
And when, amid no earthly moans,
Down, down that town shall settle hence,
Hell, rising from a thousand thrones,
Shall do it reverence.

Ralph Waldo Emerson - The Day's Ration

When I was born,
From all the seas of strength Fate filled a chalice,
Saying, This be thy portion, child; this chalice,
Less than a lily's, thou shalt daily draw
From my great arteries; nor less, nor more.
All substances the cunning chemist Time
Melts down into that liquor of my life,
Friends, foes, joys, fortunes, beauty, and disgust,
And whether I am angry or content,
Indebted or insulted, loved or hurt,
All he distils into sidereal wine,
And brims my little cup; heedless, alas!
Of all he sheds how little it will hold,
How much runs over on the desert sands.
If a new muse draw me with splendid ray,
And I uplift myself into her heaven,
The needs of the first sight absorb my blood,
And all the following hours of the day
Drag a ridiculous age.
To-day, when friends approach, and every hour
Brings book or starbright scroll of genius,
The tiny cup will hold not a bead more,
And all the costly liquor runs to waste,
Nor gives the jealous time one diamond drop
So to be husbanded for poorer days.
Why need I volumes, if one word suffice?
Why need I galleries, when a pupil's draught
After the master's sketch, fills and o'erfills
My apprehension? Why should I roam,
Who cannot circumnavigate the sea
Of thoughts and things at home, but still adjourn
The nearest matters to another moon?
Why see new men
Who have not understood the old?

Oliver Wendell Holmes - The Deacon's Masterpiece Or, The Wonderful "One-Hoss Shay": A Logical Story

Have you heard of the wonderful one-hoss shay,
That was built in such a logical way
It ran a hundred years to a day,
And then, of a sudden, it -- ah, but stay,
I'll tell you what happened without delay,
Scaring the parson into fits,
Frightening people out of their wits, --
Have you ever heard of that, I say?

Seventeen hundred and fifty-five.
Georgius Secundus was then alive, --
Snuffy old drone from the German hive.
That was the year when Lisbon-town
Saw the earth open and gulp her down,
And Braddock's army was done so brown,
Left without a scalp to its crown.
It was on the terrible Earthquake-day
That the Deacon finished the one-hoss shay.

Now in building of chaises, I tell you what,
There is always somewhere a weakest spot, --
In hub, tire, felloe, in spring or thill,
In panel, or crossbar, or floor, or sill,
In screw, bolt, thoroughbrace, -- lurking still,
Find it somewhere you must and will, --
Above or below, or within or without, --
And that's the reason, beyond a doubt,
A chaise breaks down, but does n't wear out.

But the Deacon swore (as Deacons do,
With an "I dew vum," or an "I tell yeou")
He would build one shay to beat the taown
'N' the keounty 'n' all the kentry raoun';
It should be so built that it could n' break daown:
"Fur," said the Deacon, "'t 's mighty plain

Thut the weakes' place mus' stan' the strain;
'N' the way t' fix it, uz I maintain,
Is only jest
T' make that place uz strong uz the rest."

So the Deacon inquired of the village folk
Where he could find the strongest oak,
That could n't be split nor bent nor broke, --
That was for spokes and floor and sills;
He sent for lancewood to make the thills;
The crossbars were ash, from the straightest trees,
The panels of white-wood, that cuts like cheese,
But lasts like iron for things like these;
The hubs of logs from the "Settler's ellum," --
Last of its timber, -- they could n't sell 'em,
Never an axe had seen their chips,
And the wedges flew from between their lips,
Their blunt ends frizzled like celery-tips;
Step and prop-iron, bolt and screw,
Spring, tire, axle, and linchpin too,
Steel of the finest, bright and blue;
Thoroughbrace bison-skin, thick and wide;
Boot, top, dasher, from tough old hide
Found in the pit when the tanner died.
That was the way he "put her through."
"There!" said the Deacon, "naow she'll dew!"

Do! I tell you, I rather guess
She was a wonder, and nothing less!
Colts grew horses, beards turned gray,
Deacon and deaconess dropped away,
Children and grandchildren -- where were they?
But there stood the stout old one-hoss shay
As fresh as on Lisbon-earthquake-day!

EIGHTEEN HUNDRED; -- it came and found
The Deacon's masterpiece strong and sound.
Eighteen hundred increased by ten; --
"Hahnsum kerridge" they called it then.

135

Eighteen hundred and twenty came; --
Running as usual; much the same.
Thirty and forty at last arrive,
And then come fifty, and FIFTY-FIVE.

Little of all we value here
Wakes on the morn of its hundreth year
Without both feeling and looking queer.
In fact, there's nothing that keeps its youth,
So far as I know, but a tree and truth.
(This is a moral that runs at large;
Take it. -- You're welcome. -- No extra charge.)

FIRST OF NOVEMBER, -- the Earthquake-day, --
There are traces of age in the one-hoss shay,
A general flavor of mild decay,
But nothing local, as one may say.
There could n't be, -- for the Deacon's art
Had made it so like in every part
That there was n't a chance for one to start.
For the wheels were just as strong as the thills,
And the floor was just as strong as the sills,
And the panels just as strong as the floor,
And the whipple-tree neither less nor more,
And the back crossbar as strong as the fore,
And spring and axle and hub encore.
And yet, as a whole, it is past a doubt
In another hour it will be worn out!

First of November, 'Fifty-five!
This morning the parson takes a drive.
Now, small boys, get out of the way!
Here comes the wonderful one-horse shay,
Drawn by a rat-tailed, ewe-necked bay.
"Huddup!" said the parson. -- Off went they.
The parson was working his Sunday's text, --
Had got to fifthly, and stopped perplexed
At what the -- Moses -- was coming next.
All at once the horse stood still,

Close by the meet'n'-house on the hill.
First a shiver, and then a thrill,
Then something decidedly like a spill, --
And the parson was sitting upon a rock,
At half past nine by the meet'n-house clock, --
Just the hour of the Earthquake shock!
What do you think the parson found,
When he got up and stared around?
The poor old chaise in a heap or mound,
As if it had been to the mill and ground!
You see, of course, if you're not a dunce,
How it went to pieces all at once, --
All at once, and nothing first, --
Just as bubbles do when they burst.

End of the wonderful one-hoss shay.
Logic is logic. That's all I say.

Alan Seeger - The Need to Love

The need to love that all the stars obey
Entered my heart and banished all beside.
Bare were the gardens where I used to stray;
Faded the flowers that one time satisfied.

Before the beauty of the west on fire,
The moonlit hills from cloister-casements viewed
Cloud-like arose the image of desire,
And cast out peace and maddened solitude.

I sought the City and the hopes it held:
With smoke and brooding vapors intercurled,
As the thick roofs and walls close-paralleled
Shut out the fair horizons of the world---

A truant from the fields and rustic joy,
In my changed thought that image even so
Shut out the gods I worshipped as a boy
And all the pure delights I used to know.

Often the veil has trembled at some tide
Of lovely reminiscence and revealed
How much of beauty Nature holds beside
Sweet lips that sacrifice and arms that yield:

Clouds, window-framed, beyond the huddled eaves
When summer cumulates their golden chains,
Or from the parks the smell of burning leaves,
Fragrant of childhood in the country lanes,

An organ-grinder's melancholy tune
In rainy streets, or from an attic sill
The blue skies of a windy afternoon
Where our kites climbed once from some grassy hill:

And my soul once more would be wrapped entire
In the pure peace and blessing of those years.
Before the fierce infection of Desire
Had ravaged all the flesh. Through starting tears

Shone that lost Paradise; but, if it did,
Again ere long the prison-shades would fall
That Youth condemns itself to walk amid,
So narrow, but so beautiful withal.

And I have followed Fame with less devotion,
And kept no real ambition but to see
Rise from the foam of Nature's sunlit ocean
My dream of palpable divinity;

And aught the world contends for to mine eye
Seemed not so real a meaning of success
As only once to clasp before I die
My vision of embodied happiness.

Auna Raunea

Ralph Waldo Emerson - The Park

The prosperous and beautiful
To me seem not to wear
The yoke of conscience masterful,
Which galls me everywhere.

I cannot shake off the god;
On my neck he makes his seat;
I look at my face in the glass,
My eyes his eye-balls meet.

Enchanters! enchantresses!
Your gold makes you seem wise:
The morning mist within your grounds
More proudly rolls, more softly lies.

Yet spake yon purple mountain,
Yet said yon ancient wood,
That night or day, that love or crime
Lead all souls to the Good.

Ralph Waldo Emerson - The Problem

I like a church, I like a cowl,
I love a prophet of the soul,

And on my heart monastic aisles
Fall like sweet strains or pensive smiles;
Yet not for all his faith can see,
Would I that cowled churchman be.
Why should the vest on him allure,
Which I could not on me endure?

Not from a vain or shallow thought
His awful Jove young Phidias brought;
Never from lips of cunning fell
The thrilling Delphic oracle;
Out from the heart of nature rolled
The burdens of the Bible old;
The litanies of nations came,
Like the volcano's tongue of flame,
Up from the burning core below,
The canticles of love and woe.
The hand that rounded Peter's dome,
And groined the aisles of Christian Rome,
Wrought in a sad sincerity,
Himself from God he could not free;
He builded better than he knew,
The conscious stone to beauty grew.

Know'st thou what wove yon woodbird's nest
Of leaves and feathers from her breast;
Or how the fish outbuilt its shell,
Painting with morn each annual cell;
Or how the sacred pine tree adds
To her old leaves new myriads?
Such and so grew these holy piles,
Whilst love and terror laid the tiles.
Earth proudly wears the Parthenon
As the best gem upon her zone;
And Morning opes with haste her lids
To gaze upon the Pyramids;
O'er England's abbeys bends the sky
As on its friends with kindred eye;
For out of Thought's interior sphere
These wonders rose to upper air,
And nature gladly gave them place,
Adopted them into her race,
And granted them an equal date
With Andes and with Ararat.

These temples grew as grows the grass,
Art might obey but not surpass.
The passive Master lent his hand
To the vast soul that o'er him planned,
And the same power that reared the shrine,
Bestrode the tribes that knelt within.
Even the fiery Pentecost
Girds with one flame the Countless host,
Trances the heart through chanting quires,
And through the priest the mind inspires.

The word unto the prophet spoken
Was writ on tables yet unbroken;
The word by seers or sibyls told
In groves of oak, or fanes of gold,
Still floats upon the morning wind,
Still whispers to the willing mind.
One accent of the Holy Ghost
The heedless world hath never lost.

I know what say the Fathers wise,
The Book itself before me lies,
Old Chrysostom, best Augustine,
And he who blent both in his line,
The younger Golden-lips or mines,
Taylor, the Shakspeare of divines,
His words are music in my ear,
I see his cowled portrait dear,
And yet for all his faith could see,
I would not the good bishop be.

Auna Raunea

Ralph Waldo Emerson - The Rhodora
On Being Asked, Whence Is The Flower?

In May, when sea-winds pierced our solitudes,
I found the fresh Rhodora in the woods,
Spreading its leafless blooms in a damp nook,
To please the desert and the sluggish brook.
The purple petals, fallen in the pool,
Made the black water with their beauty gay;
Here might the red-bird come his plumes to cool,
And court the flower that cheapens his array.
Rhodora! if the sages ask thee why
This charm is wasted on the earth and sky,
Tell them, dear, that if eyes were made for seeing,
Then Beauty is its own excuse for being:
Why thou wert there, O rival of the rose!
I never thought to ask, I never knew:
But, in my simple ignorance, suppose
The self-same Power that brought me there brought you.

Joyce Kilmer - The Singing Girl

(For the Rev. Edward F. Garesche, S. J.)

There was a little maiden
In blue and silver drest,
She sang to God in Heaven
And God within her breast.
It flooded me with pleasure,
It pierced me like a sword,
When this young maiden sang: "My soul
Doth magnify the Lord."
The stars sing all together
And hear the angels sing,
But they said they had never heard
So beautiful a thing.
Saint Mary and Saint Joseph,
And Saint Elizabeth,
Pray for us poets now
And at the hour of death.

Ralph Waldo Emerson - The Snow-Storm

Announced by all the trumpets of the sky,
Arrives the snow, and, driving o'er the fields,
Seems nowhere to alight: the whited air
Hides hill and woods, the river, and the heaven,
And veils the farmhouse at the garden's end.
The sled and traveller stopped, the courier's feet
Delated, all friends shut out, the housemates sit
Around the radiant fireplace, enclosed
In a tumultuous privacy of storm.
Come see the north wind's masonry.
Out of an unseen quarry evermore
Furnished with tile, the fierce artificer
Curves his white bastions with projected roof
Round every windward stake, or tree, or door.
Speeding, the myriad-handed, his wild work
So fanciful, so savage, nought cares he
For number or proportion. Mockingly,
On coop or kennel he hangs Parian wreaths;
A swan-like form invests the hiddden thorn;
Fills up the famer's lane from wall to wall,
Maugre the farmer's sighs; and at the gate
A tapering turret overtops the work.
And when his hours are numbered, and the world
Is all his own, retiring, as he were not,
Leaves, when the sun appears, astonished Art
To mimic in slow structures, stone by stone,
Built in an age, the mad wind's night-work,
The frolic architecture of the snow.

Ralph Waldo Emerson - The Sphinx

The Sphinx is drowsy,
Her wings are furled:
Her ear is heavy,
She broods on the world.
"Who'll tell me my secret,
The ages have kept?__
I awaited the seer
While they slumbered and slept:__
"The fate of the man-child,
The meaning of man;
Known fruit of the unknown;
Daedalian plan;
Out of sleeping a waking,
Out of waking a sleep;
Life death overtaking;
Deep underneath deep?

:Erect as a sunbeam,
Upspringeth the palm;
The elephant browses,
Undaunted and calm;
In beautiful motion
The thrush plies his wings;
Kind leaves of his covert,
Your silence he sings.

"The waves, unashaméd,
In difference sweet,
Play glad with the breezes,
Old playfellows meet;
The journeying atoms,
Primordial wholes,
Firmly draw, firmly drive,
By their animate poles.

Auna Raunea

"Sea, earth, air, sound, silence,
Plant, quadruped, bird,
By one music enchanted,
One deity stirred,--
Each the other adorning,
Accompany still;
Night veileth the morning,
The vapor the hill.

"The babe by its mother
Lies bathéd in joy;
Glide its hours uncounted,--
The sun is its toy;
Shines the peace of all being,
Without cloud, in its eyes;
And the sum of the world
In soft miniature lies.

"But man crouches and blushes,
Absconds and conceals;
He creepeth and peepeth,
He palters and steals;
Infirm, melancholy,
Jealous glancing around,
An oaf, an accomplice,
He poisons the ground.

"Out spoke the great mother,
Beholding his fear;--
At the sound of her accents
Cold shuddered the sphere:--
'Who has drugged my boy's cup?
Who has mixed my boy's bread?
Who, with sadness and madness,
Has turned my child's head?

I heard a poet answer
Aloud and cheerfully,
"Say on, sweet Sphinx! thy dirges
Are pleasant songs to me.
Deep love lieth under
These pictures of time;
They fade in the light of
Their meaning sublime.

"The fiend that man harries
Is love of the Best;
Yawns the pit of the Dragon,
Lit by rays from the Blest.
The lethe of Nature
Can't trance him again,
Whose soul sees the perfect,
Which his eyes seek in vain.

"To vision profounder,
Man's spirit must dive;
His aye-rolling orb
At no goal will arrive;
The heavens that now draw him
With sweetness untold,
Once found,--for new heavens
He spurneth the old.

"Pride ruined the angels,
Their shame them restores;
Lurks the joy that is sweetest
In stings of remorse.
Have I a lover
Who is noble and free?--
I would he were nobler
Than to love me.

"Eterne alternation
Now follows, now flies;
And under pain, pleasure,--

Auna Raunea

Under pleasure, pain lies.
Love works at the center,
Heart-heaving alway;
Forth speed the strong pulses
To the borders of day.

"Dull Sphinx, Jove keep thy five wits'
Thy sight is growing blear;
Rue, myrrh and cummin for the Sphinx,
Her muddy eyes to clear!"
The old Sphinx bit her thick lip,--
Said, "Who taught thee me to name?
I am thy spirit, yoke-fellow;
Of thine eye I am eyebeam.

"Thou art the unanswered question;
Couldst see thy proper eye,
Alway it asketh, asketh;
And each answer is a lie.
So take thy question through nature,
It through thousand natures ply;
Ask on, thou clothed eternity;
Time is the false reply.

Uprose the merry Sphinx,
And crouched no more in stone;
She melted into purple cloud,
She silvered in the moon;
She spired into a yellow flame;
She flowered in blossoms red;
She flowed into a foaming wave:
She stood Monadnoc's head.

Through a thousand voices
Spoke the universal dame
"Who telleth one of my meanings
Is master of all I am."

Joyce Kilmer - The Thorn

(For the Rev. Charles L. O'Donnell, C. S. C.)

The garden of God is a radiant place,
And every flower has a holy face:
Our Lady like a lily bends above the cloudy sod,
But Saint Michael is the thorn on the rosebush of God.
David is the song upon God's lips,
And Our Lady is the goblet that He sips:
And Gabriel's the breath of His command,
But Saint Michael is the sword in God's right hand.
The Ivory Tower is fair to see,
And may her walls encompass me!
But when the Devil comes with the thunder of his might,
Saint Michael, show me how to fight!

Oliver Wendell Holmes - The Two Streams

Behold the rocky wall
That down its sloping sides
Pours the swift rain-drops, blending, as they fall,
In rushing river-tides!
Yon stream, whose sources run
Turned by a pebble's edge,
Is Athabasca, rolling toward the sun
Through the cleft mountain-ledge.
The slender rill had strayed,
But for the slanting stone,
To evening's ocean, with the tangled braid
Of foam-flecked Oregon.

So from the heights of Will
Life's parting stream descends,
And, as a moment turns its slender rill,
Each widening torrent bends, --

From the same cradle's side,
From the same mother's knee, --
One to long darkness and the frozen tide,
One to the Peaceful Sea!

Alan Seeger - The Wanderer

To see the clouds his spirit yearned toward so
Over new mountains piled and unploughed waves,
Back of old-storied spires and architraves
To watch Arcturus rise or Fomalhaut,

And roused by street-cries in strange tongues when day
Flooded with gold some domed metropolis,
Between new towers to waken and new bliss
Spread on his pillow in a wondrous way:

These were his joys. Oft under bulging crates,
Coming to market with his morning load,
The peasant found him early on his road
To greet the sunrise at the city-gates,---

There where the meadows waken in its rays,
Golden with mist, and the great roads commence,
And backward, where the chimney-tops are dense,
Cathedral-arches glimmer through the haze.

White dunes that breaking show a strip of sea,
A plowman and his team against the blue
Swiss pastures musical with cowbells, too,
And poplar-lined canals in Picardie,

And coast-towns where the vultures back and forth
Sail in the clear depths of the tropic sky,
And swallows in the sunset where they fly
Over gray Gothic cities in the north,

And the wine-cellar and the chorus there,
The dance-hall and a face among the crowd,---
Were all delights that made him sing aloud
For joy to sojourn in a world so fair.

Auna Raunea

Back of his footsteps as he journeyed fell
Range after range; ahead blue hills emerged.
Before him tireless to applaud it surged
The sweet interminable spectacle.

And like the west behind a sundown sea
Shone the past joys his memory retraced,
And bright as the blue east he always faced
Beckoned the loves and joys that were to be.

From every branch a blossom for his brow
He gathered, singing down Life's flower-lined road,
And youth impelled his spirit as he strode
Like winged Victory on the galley's prow.

That Loveliness whose being sun and star,
Green Earth and dawn and amber evening robe,
That lamp whereof the opalescent globe
The season's emulative splendors are,

That veiled divinity whose beams transpire
From every pore of universal space,
As the fair soul illumes the lovely face---
That was his guest, his passion, his desire.

His heart the love of Beauty held as hides
One gem most pure a casket of pure gold.
It was too rich a lesser thing to bold;
It was not large enough for aught besides.

Ralph Waldo Emerson - Threnody

The south-wind brings
Life, sunshine, and desire,
And on every mount and meadow
Breathes aromatic fire,
But over the dead he has no power,
The lost, the lost he cannot restore,
And, looking over the hills, I mourn
The darling who shall not return.

I see my empty house,
I see my trees repair their boughs,
And he, —the wondrous child,
Whose silver warble wild
Outvalued every pulsing sound
Within the air's cerulean round,
The hyacinthine boy, for whom
Morn well might break, and April bloom,
The gracious boy, who did adorn
The world whereinto he was born,
And by his countenance repay
The favor of the loving Day,
Has disappeared from the Day's eye;
Far and wide she cannot find him,
My hopes pursue, they cannot bind him.
Returned this day the south-wind searches
And finds young pines and budding birches,
But finds not the budding man;
Nature who lost him, cannot remake him;
Fate let him fall, Fate can't retake him;
Nature, Fate, men, him seek in vain.

And whither now, my truant wise and sweet,
Oh, whither tend thy feet?
I had the right, few days ago,
Thy steps to watch, thy place to know;
How have I forfeited the right?

Auna Raunea

Hast thou forgot me in a new delight?
I hearken for thy household cheer,
O eloquent child!
Whose voice, an equal messenger,
Conveyed thy meaning mild.
What though the pains and joys
Whereof it spoke were toys
Fitting his age and ken;—
Yet fairest dames and bearded men,
Who heard the sweet request
So gentle, wise, and grave,
Bended with joy to his behest,
And let the world's affairs go by,
Awhile to share his cordial game,
Or mend his wicker wagon frame,
Still plotting how their hungry ear
That winsome voice again might hear,
For his lips could well pronounce
Words that were persuasions.

Gentlest guardians marked serene
His early hope, his liberal mien,
Took counsel from his guiding eyes
To make this wisdom earthly wise.
Ah! vainly do these eyes recall
The school-march, each day's festival,
When every morn my bosom glowed
To watch the convoy on the road;—
The babe in willow wagon closed,
With rolling eyes and face composed,
With children forward and behind,
Like Cupids studiously inclined,
And he, the Chieftain, paced beside,
The centre of the troop allied,
With sunny face of sweet repose,
To guard the babe from fancied foes,
The little Captain innocent

Took the eye with him as he went,
Each village senior paused to scan
And speak the lovely caravan.

From the window I look out
To mark thy beautiful parade
Stately marching in cap and coat
To some tune by fairies played;
A music heard by thee alone
To works as noble led thee on.
Now love and pride, alas, in vain,
Up and down their glances strain.
The painted sled stands where it stood,
The kennel by the corded wood,
The gathered sticks to stanch the wall
Of the snow-tower, when snow should fall,
The ominous hole he dug in the sand,
And childhood's castles built or planned.
His daily haunts I well discern,
The poultry yard, the shed, the barn,
And every inch of garden ground
Paced by the blessed feet around,
From the road-side to the brook;
Whereinto he loved to look.
Step the meek birds where erst they ranged,
The wintry garden lies unchanged,
The brook into the stream runs on,
But the deep-eyed Boy is gone.

On that shaded day,
Dark with more clouds than tempests are,
When thou didst yield thy innocent breath
In bird-like heavings unto death,
Night came, and Nature had not thee,—
I said, we are mates in misery.
The morrow dawned with needless glow,
Each snow-bird chirped, each fowl must crow,
Each tramper started,— but the feet
Of the most beautiful and sweet

Of human youth had left the hill
And garden,—they were bound and still,
There's not a sparrow or a wren,
There's not a blade of autumn grain,
Which the four seasons do not tend,
And tides of life and increase lend,
And every chick of every bird,
And weed and rock-moss is preferred.
O ostriches' forgetfulness!
O loss of larger in the less!
Was there no star that could be sent,
No watcher in the firmament,
No angel from the countless host,
That loiters round the crystal coast,
Could stoop to heal that only child,
Nature's sweet marvel undefiled,
And keep the blossom of the earth,
Which all her harvests were not worth?
Not mine, I never called thee mine,
But nature's heir,— if I repine,
And, seeing rashly torn and moved,
Not what I made, but what I loved.
Grow early old with grief that then
Must to the wastes of nature go,—
'Tis because a general hope
Was quenched, and all must doubt and grope
For flattering planets seemed to say,
This child should ills of ages stay,—
By wondrous tongue and guided pen
Bring the flown muses back to men. —
Perchance, not he, but nature ailed,
The world, and not the infant failed,
It was not ripe yet, to sustain
A genius of so fine a strain,
Who gazed upon the sun and moon
As if he came unto his own,
And pregnant with his grander thought,
Brought the old order into doubt.
Awhile his beauty their beauty tried,

They could not feed him, and he died,
And wandered backward as in scorn
To wait an Æon to be born.
Ill day which made this beauty waste;
Plight broken, this high face defaced!
Some went and came about the dead,
And some in books of solace read,
Some to their friends the tidings say,
Some went to write, some went to pray,
One tarried here, there hurried one,
But their heart abode with none.
Covetous death bereaved us all
To aggrandize one funeral.
The eager Fate which carried thee
Took the largest part of me.
For this losing is true dying,
This is lordly man's down-lying,
This is slow but sure reclining,
Star by star his world resigning.

O child of Paradise!
Boy who made dear his father's home
In whose deep eyes
Men read the welfare of the times to come;
I am too much bereft;
The world dishonored thou hast left;
O truths and natures costly lie;
O trusted, broken prophecy!
O richest fortune sourly crossed;
Born for the future, to the future lost!

The deep Heart answered, Weepest thou?
Worthier cause for passion wild,
If I had not taken the child.
And deemest thou as those who pore
With aged eyes short way before?
Think'st Beauty vanished from the coast
Of matter, and thy darling lost?
Taught he not thee, — the man of eld,

Auna Raunea

Whose eyes within his eyes beheld
Heaven's numerous hierarchy span
The mystic gulf from God to man?
To be alone wilt thou begin,
When worlds of lovers hem thee in?
To-morrow, when the masks shall fall
That dizen nature's carnival,
The pure shall see, by their own will,
Which overflowing love shall fill,—
'Tis not within the force of Fate
The fate-conjoined to separate.
But thou, my votary, weepest thou?
I gave thee sight, where is it now?
I taught thy heart beyond the reach
Of ritual, Bible, or of speech;
Wrote in thy mind's transparent table
As far as the incommunicable;
Taught thee each private sign to raise
Lit by the supersolar blaze.
Past utterance and past belief,
And past the blasphemy of grief,
The mysteries of nature's heart,—
And though no muse can these impart,
Throb thine with nature's throbbing breast,
And all is clear from east to west.

I came to thee as to a friend,
Dearest, to thee I did not send
Tutors, but a joyful eye,
Innocence that matched the sky,
Lovely locks a form of wonder,
Laughter rich as woodland thunder;
That thou might'st entertain apart
The richest flowering of all art;
And, as the great all-loving Day
Through smallest chambers takes its way,
That thou might'st break thy daily bread
With Prophet, Saviour, and head;
That thou might'st cherish for thine own

160

The riches of sweet Mary's Son,
Boy-Rabbi, Israel's Paragon:
And thoughtest thou such guest
Would in thy hall take up his rest?
Would rushing life forget its laws,
Fate's glowing revolution pause?
High omens ask diviner guess,
Not to be conned to tediousness.
And know, my higher gifts unbind
The zone that girds the incarnate mind,
When the scanty shores are full
With Thought's perilous whirling pool,
When frail Nature can no more,—
Then the spirit strikes the hour,
My servant Death with solving rite
Pours finite into infinite.
Wilt thou freeze love's tidal flow,
Whose streams through nature circling go?
Nail the star struggling to its track
On the half-climbed Zodiack?
Light is light which radiates,
Blood is blood which circulates,
Life is life which generates,
And many-seeming life is one,—
Wilt thou transfix and make it none,
Its onward stream too starkly pent
In figure, bone, and lineament?

Wilt thou uncalled interrogate
Talker! the unreplying fate?
Nor see the Genius of the whole
Ascendant in the private soul,
Beckon it when to go and come,
Self-announced its hour of doom.
Fair the soul's recess and shrine,
Magic-built, to last a season,
Masterpiece of love benign!
Fairer than expansive reason
Whose omen 'tis, and sign.

Wilt thou not ope this heart to know
What rainbows teach and sunsets show,
Verdict which accumulates
From lengthened scroll of human fates,
Voice of earth to earth returned,
Prayers of heart that inly burned;
Saying, what is excellent,
As God lives, is permanent
Hearts are dust, hearts' loves remain,
Heart's love will meet thee again.
Revere the Maker; fetch thine eye
Up to His style, and manners of the sky.
Not of adamant and gold
Built He heaven stark and cold,
No, but a nest of bending reeds,
Flowering grass and scented weeds,
Or like a traveller's fleeting tent,
Or bow above the tempest pent,
Built of tears and sacred flames,
And virtue reaching to its aims;
Built of furtherance and pursuing,
Not of spent deeds, but of doing.
Silent rushes the swift Lord
Through ruined systems still restored,
Broad-sowing, bleak and void to bless,
Plants with worlds the wilderness,
Waters with tears of ancient sorrow
Apples of Eden ripe to-morrow;
House and tenant go to ground,
Lost in God, in Godhead found.

Ralph Waldo Emerson - Two Rivers

Thy summer voice, Musketaquit,
Repeats the music of the rain;
But sweeter rivers pulsing flit
Through thee, as thou through the Concord Plain.
Thou in thy narrow banks art pent:
The stream I love unbounded goes
Through flood and sea and firmament;
Through light, through life, it forward flows.

I see the inundation sweet,
I hear the spending of the steam
Through years, through men, through Nature fleet,
Through love and thought, through power and dream.

Musketaquit, a goblin strong,
Of shard and flint makes jewels gay;
They lose their grief who hear his song,
And where he winds is the day of day.

So forth and brighter fares my stream,--
Who drink it shall not thirst again;
No darkness taints its equal gleam,
And ages drop in it like rain.

Oliver Wendell Holmes - Under the Violets

HER hands are cold; her face is white;
No more her pulses come and go;
Her eyes are shut to life and light;--
Fold the white vesture, snow on snow,
And lay her where the violets blow.

But not beneath a graven stone,
To plead for tears with alien eyes;
A slender cross of wood alone
Shall say, that here a maiden lies
In peace beneath the peaceful skies.

And gray old trees of hugest limb
Shall wheel their circling shadows round
To make the scorching sunlight dim
That drinks the greenness from the ground,
And drop their dead leaves on her mound.

When o'er their boughs the squirrels run,
And through their leaves the robins call,
And, ripening in the autumn sun,
The acorns and the chestnuts fall,
Doubt not that she will heed them all.

For her the morning choir shall sing
Its matins from the branches high,
And every minstrel-voice of Spring,
That trills beneath the April sky,
Shall greet her with its earliest cry.

When, turning round their dial-track,
Eastward the lengthening shadows pass,
Her little mourners, clad in black,
The crickets, sliding through the grass,
Shall pipe for her an evening mass.

At last the rootlets of the trees
Shall find the prison where she lies,
And bear the buried dust they seize
In leaves and blossoms to the skies.
So may the soul that warmed it rise!

If any, born of kindlier blood,
Should ask, What maiden lies below?
Say only this: A tender bud,
That tried to blossom in the snow,
Lies withered where the violets blow.

Oliver Wendell Holmes - Union and Liberty

FLAG of the heroes who left us their glory,
Borne through their battle-fields' thunder and flame,
Blazoned in song and illumined in story,
Wave o'er us all who inherit their fame!

Up with our banner bright,
Sprinkled with starry light,
Spread its fair emblems from mountain to shore,
While through the sounding sky
Loud rings the Nation's cry,
UNION AND LIBERTY! ONE EVERMORE!

Light of our firmament, guide of our Nation,
Pride of her children, and honored afar,
Let the wide beams of thy full constellation
Scatter each cloud that would darken a star!

Up with our banner bright,
Sprinkled with starry light,
Spread its fair emblems from mountain to shore,
While through the sounding sky
Loud rings the Nation's cry,
UNION AND LIBERTY! ONE EVERMORE!

Empire unsceptred! what foe shall assail thee,
Bearing the standard of Liberty's van?
Think not the God of thy fathers shall fail thee,
Striving with men for the birthright of man!

Up with our banner bright,
Sprinkled with starry light,
Spread its fair emblems from mountain to shore,
While through the sounding sky
Loud rings the Nation's cry,
UNION AND LIBERTY! ONE EVERMORE!

Yet if, by madness and treachery blighted,
Dawns the dark hour when the sword thou must draw,
Then with the arms of thy millions united,
Smite the bold traitors to Freedom and Law!

Up with our banner bright,
Sprinkled with starry light,
Spread its fair emblems from mountain to shore,
While through the sounding sky
Loud rings the Nation's cry,
UNION AND LIBERTY! ONE EVERMORE!

Lord of the Universe! shield us and guide us,
Trusting Thee always, through shadow and sun!
Thou hast united us, who shall divide us?
Keep us, oh keep us the MANY IN ONE!

Up with our banner bright,
Sprinkled with starry light,
Spread its fair emblems from mountain to shore,
While through the sounding sky
Loud rings the Nation's cry,
UNION AND LIBERTY! ONE EVERMORE!

Joyce Kilmer - Vision
(For Aline)

Homer, they tell us, was blind and could not see the beautiful
faces
Looking up into his own and reflecting the joy of his dream,
Yet did he seem
Gifted with eyes that could follow the gods to their holiest places.
I have no vision of gods, not of Eros with love-arrows laden,
Jupiter thundering death or of Juno his white-breasted queen,
Yet have I seen
All of the joy of the world in the innocent heart of a maiden.